C000318431

Acclaim for *Warriors, Settlers & Nomads:*

When I started reading **Warriors, Settlers & Nomads** by Terence Watts, it gripped me more than any other self-help book I've ever read. The author's theory is validated by the history of the human race itself! While I already had some clues as to how the historical groups influence my behaviour, I still found myself taking the personality test with extreme curiosity. Then the author's writing style kept me glued to the pages long enough to be late for an appointment, which is quite rare for me.

I strongly recommend this book to anyone on the road to greater awareness or self-empowerment.

– **Roy Hunter MS**, author of *The Art of Hypnosis*
and *Master the Power of Self-Hypnosis*

Once in a generation, a work of genius is discovered that you know instinctively will become mainstream and assimilated into modern culture. *Warriors, Settlers & Nomads* is such a work of genius.

Warriors, Settlers & Nomads can transform your life. It's a radically different approach to personalty development and enlightenment. Terence Watts invites you to discover the qualities of your tribe and your predominant personality type, e.g. are you a Warrior, Settler or Nomad, or a combination of all three? Rediscovering my lost tribe has not only enabled me to uncover lost truth about my personality type, but it has also been the most meaningful experience in self analysis.

This book is, I believe, the first ever simple-to-use guide to our personalities, helping us to understand our psychological state through the inherent characteristics represented in our primeval forbears. This book explains why people do what they do in life, and helps you resolve life's issues, develop a healthy self-concept, enhance relationships and careers, and fulfil your goals in an easier way. It gives you freedom to express your true personality.

Terence Watts is to be congratulated for his contribution to modern psychology and for pointing us in the direction of our roots in order to become truly free in expressing our personalities today.

– **Joseph Keaney PhD, DPsych, BA, DCH,**
Director, Institute of Clinical Hypnotherapy & Psychotherapy,
Cork City, Ireland

Warriors, Settlers & Nomads

Discovering **Who We Are**
& **What We Can Be**

Terence Watts

Crown House Publishing Limited
www.crownhouse.co.uk

First published in the UK by

Crown House Publishing Limited
Crown Buildings
Bancyfelin
Carmarthen
Wales
SA33 5ND
UK

www.crownhouse.co.uk

© Terence Watts 2000

The right of Terence Watts to be identified as the author of this work
has been asserted by him in accordance with the Copyright, Designs
and Patents Act 1988.

Reprinted 2001 (twice), 2004, 2006.

All rights reserved. Except as permitted under current
legislation no part of this work may be photocopied, stored in a retrieval
system, published, performed in public, adapted, broadcast, transmitted,
recorded or reproduced in any form or by any means, without the prior
permission of the copyright owners. Enquiries should be addressed to
Crown House Publishing Limited.

British Library of Cataloguing-in-Publication Data
A catalogue entry for this book is available
from the British Library.

10-digit ISBN 1899836489
13-digit ISBN 978-189983648-2

LCCN 2004116148

Printed and bound in the UK by
Antony Rowe Ltd
Chippenham

To 'Measle',
the ever-constant and limitless source of my
drive and inspiration.

Table of Contents

Acknowledgements

I would like to thank the following people for their wisdom and help; all of them contributed much that allowed this book to come into being: Kevin Hogan; Wendi Friesen; Marcia Proctor; Joe Keaney; Neil French; Rita Stanley; Bridget Shine; Matt Pearce; all my friends and colleagues at home and abroad, for their patience in answering and re-answering myriad questions and tests.

Foreword

Your present environment.
Your personal history.
Your genetic make-up.

These three elements determine who you are and how you behave at any moment in time. Scientific research has shown that this is true beyond question. How significant are these three elements?

Research into genetics has clearly shown that everything from body weight to IQ is positively correlated to your genes. Obese parents tend to give birth to children who will ultimately become obese. This tendency holds true even when these children are raised in other homes. There are genetic predispositions to some forms of cancer, psychological disorders, criminal behaviour and even divorce. Don't think that there is a "divorce gene" because there isn't! There are a number of genes that interact (polygenetically) that influence behaviour in such a way to increase the likelihood of divorce. Your genes influence who you are and how you behave in ways you can only begin to imagine.

Meanwhile...there is a mountain of research that clearly shows that the environment we inhabit from moment to moment strongly influences our behaviour. Many years ago a study was done where students either took on the role of prisoners or prison guards in a university building. Within hours the students in the role of prison guards were physically abusing those who had been assigned the role of prisoners. Otherwise normal students, no different to you and me, were physically lashing out at other innocent students. In the United States you will often see fans at a professional football game throwing snowballs at referees. This is surprising to some because the people who are close enough to throw snowballs are those who can afford the front row seats! The wealthy, sophisticated and most upstanding members of the community are those who are transformed by the crowd – their current environment. Thus the environment we are in determines in large part who we are and how we behave.

Finally, your personal history is a very important influence on who you are and how you behave. We tend to act consistently with our past actions, whatever they were. We also are subjects of stimulus-response experiences that include being attracted to a type of person, experiencing phobias, having likes and dislikes, and so on. You are, in large part, a summation of your personal history. Your life is a story that is being written and has many possible interpretations and endings. Your interpretation of your life story influences your behaviour at this very moment.

These are the three basic elements that have blended to bring you to where you are today. Or are they? Now something interesting has happened. You have picked up a copy of *Warriors, Settlers & Nomads* by Terence Watts. This tells me a little bit about who you are. It tells me that you are interested in who you are and where you are going. You are someone who is curious. You desire to understand human nature. You want to create change in your life and those of others and you are serious about it.

Warriors, Settlers & Nomads is a handbook for understanding your life and creating the future you so richly deserve. Terence Watts takes you on a wonderful journey through his fascinating extension of the theory of evolutionary psychology. He believes that the three key influences on our current behaviour were that of the Warriors, the Settlers and the Nomads...and I think he might be right.

You will enjoy the process of self discovery as you take the personality test at the beginning of the book and you will begin to see those around you in a very different light, as you consider how they came to be who they are. You are about to learn about how to let go of the limitations of your early years. You will also discover new strategies for creating a future that will change your life forever. *Warriors, Settlers & Nomads* is more than a self help book. This book helps you understand who you are and how you came to be "you"! Finally, Terence Watts gives you the most powerful tools available to create the changes you want. You will learn the powerful skills of self hypnosis and visualization.

This book is a treasure trove of useful and life-changing strategies. Enjoy it, and let it change your world!

Kevin Hogan PhD

Author of *The Psychology of Persuasion*
and *Through the Open Door: Secrets of Self Hypnosis*
Minnesota Institute of Hypnosis and Hypnotherapy
1960 Cliff Lake Rd. #112-200
Eagan, MN 55122
www.kevinhogan.com

Preface

You should not dismiss any part of what you read in this book without first trying it – and genuinely suspending scepticism, cynicism, or any feeling of 'knowing' it could not work for you while you do so. Those feelings are a part of your problem, a part of why you are not yet where you want to be.

Forget about those individuals who boast that they can trace their ancestry back as far as William the Conqueror, or the Domesday Book. The fact is, we *all* have origins going right back through time, way beyond the Domesday Book. Beyond the Pharaohs and the ancient Greeks... right back beyond recorded history... back at least to the dawning of our own particular species, *Homo sapiens*.

It doesn't matter at all whether your own particular lineage can be traced back through two or three generations or a thousand years. A thousand years is but a mere fraction of your ancestral line. Archaeologists have recently pin-pointed the actual cave in Africa where the first members of our race lived between a hundred thousand and one hundred and fifty thousand years ago. Astonishingly, perhaps, it is believed that every one of us is descended from this small group, whose DNA was the same as our own still is, but different from those that had gone before them.

At first, this new race shared the planet with an apparently unrelated and less intelligent species of man, the Neanderthal. But they disappeared without trace, except for a few fossilised remains, some thirty thousand years ago. So now homo sapiens stands alone as probably the most successful primate that has so far existed on Earth. Genetic tests prove the closeness of the relationship of all the races of modern man, regardless of apparent level of intellectual, physical or emotional development – many races, but only one species.

For many tens of thousands of years, these new humans hardly changed their way of life, if at all. Nomadic creatures wandering far and wide, hunter-gatherers living in small packs, surviving by their wits and ingenuity. But then... civilisation happened, a civilisation peopled by a race that carried, and still carries, the sometimes savage but also intensely powerful ancestral memories and instincts of their forebears.

Not every scientist or psychologist agrees with this notion that evolution has a bearing upon our personality and 'way of being'; there are many who still insist that nurture, rather than nature, governs the way we are. In other words, they believe that it is our upbringing, rather than our genetics, that shape our personality as an individual. Yet, when you discover the astounding similarities between the lives of identical twins who have been separated at birth and brought up independently – maybe even on opposite sides of the world – you can only marvel at the power of inheritance. More and more, psychologists and others who are interested in human behaviour are becoming engrossed in the science of psychological evolution; more and more, they finding evidence that the human mind has developed in a certain way for precisely the same reason as has the physical body – to ensure the survival of the individuals most adapted to their environment. In some way or another, such development is passed on to each new generation, ensuring a steady progress towards... but who knows what or where?

There is abundant proof of this existence of inherited memories in other species besides humans. Eels find their way to their breeding grounds in the Sargasso sea, even though they have never been there before; turtles, upon hatching from their eggs, clamber out of the sand and race for the water, for the sea offers life while the sand does not. And how about this? Teach a rat to find its way through a maze and its offspring will learn the route faster. And after a few generations of learning, the offspring seem almost to know the maze without having to learn it at all.

But what of our own race? Well, the more warlike of those early tribes would have encouraged and taught warlike behaviour, for that is exactly how they survived – by dominance. Dominance over those with whom they came into contact and dominance within the tribe itself creating a hierarchy wherein the strongest and quickest had the highest chance of survival. But the more peaceful individuals would have encouraged harmony, because that is how *their* world worked, a common bond and shared strengths allowing them to survive in a harsh and unyielding environment.

For many years, the two types would have had little contact. The Earth was a big place and the human tribes remained constantly on the move, the more peaceful no doubt avoiding the more war-like... until that day that civilisation dawned and the race began to cease its wandering.

The New World soon threw into sharp relief the three distinct personalities that had been latent within their numbers – the Warriors, the Nomads and the Settlers. Those same three types still exist today, each with their own inborn strengths, instincts and weaknesses, each with its inherited potential for success. Most of us, though, never become aware of any such inheritance and as a result, it lies unused and withering.

When you discover which of the three you are, you will be able to set free the dormant resources within you, and capitalise on strengths and abilities you may not yet even realise you possess. You will be able to tune in to the success-oriented wisdom of the ancients, a wisdom that is your birthright and which can lead you unerringly to whatever it is that you seek. If you have ever felt that there must be more to life, then you are probably right – and this book lays bare the secret of how to find it!

Chapter One
Our Ancestral Memories

I make no apology for the fact that this book quite often shows a cheerful disregard for the history of the human race as it is usually taught. It is not intended as a history book; it is a self-help book, based on the known evolution of the human psyche and an understanding of what must have gone before us. It is designed to help you identify and use inherited resources within yourself that you may not otherwise have even realised that you possessed. These resources can help you attain your goals, fulfil your desires, and generally be... a success!

Terence Watts

The human species as we know it has existed for around one hundred thousand years. Throughout that time, there have been two separate strains of genetic information being passed from one generation to another, through different countries and cultures, through plague and famine, not stopped nor even hindered by barbarian uprisings, religious crusades or bloody revolutions.

Those two genetic strains continued relentlessly, actually gaining strength, through times of witches and warlocks, peasants and kings, knights and serfs; they survived wars, continent-splitting earthquakes, mammoth volcanic upheavals, holocaust, terrorism and fantastic inventions, until, in one split second in time, they fused together in a single human cell that was to become... YOU!

A Special Moment

In that very moment of conception, the genetically coded DNA strands from each of your parents combined, ensuring that you became a living record of the lives and ways of your ancestors. And we are not just talking about the way you look – we are talking about your ancestral memory, the complete set of instincts and response patterns that were responsible for the survival of those two genetic streams in the first place. We are talking about the biological memory traces of attitudes towards success and survival that are every bit as relevant today as they were then.

1

The *real you.* The you that you were actually born to be.

This is the real you, whom even you do not know yet! Because from the moment you were born, every experience, every living moment, had its effect upon that basic personality, moulding, shaping, developing... distorting. Some of that distortion was useful, leading to the development of required social behaviour and conscience, for example, and to a general understanding of your environment and how it works. But some of it was distinctly *un*helpful – created by the 'hang-ups', anxieties, idiosyncrasies and occasional cussedness of your parents and others with whom you came into contact.

At first, you had no way of knowing that what you experienced, what you were taught, was not necessarily the way that life was always going to be; you took it all on board as being 'normal' and learned to expect it, whether it was good or bad, true or false. Had you been told that the grass was blue and the sky was green, you would have believed it! Why would you not? You had no way of knowing that it was not so, no reason to doubt what you had been told, and no way of knowing that the rest of the world thought differently. And you would have vigorously resisted, at first, all attempts by others, later on, to correct that belief.

Now, that may be a rather extreme example, but it is perfectly valid. So you might begin to wonder, just how many other ideas and concepts you may be carrying that have never been corrected simply because they have never been challenged. They might well be less obvious ideas than in that example, but they could be infinitely more important. Ideas about life and living. Ideas about people. Ideas about your own family.

Ideas about yourself.

The Centre of Everything...

Before you dismiss the notion that you could have many faulty ideas or beliefs about yourself or the world you live in and the people that share it with you, consider *this* radical statement:

The Sun and stars move around the Earth, and therefore Earth is the centre of the universe.

Now, you probably instantly dismissed that idea. Everybody knows that the Earth moves around the Sun, right? Well, less than four hundred years ago, everyone did *not* know it. In fact, early in the seventeenth century, the famous astronomer Galileo was tried by the Church for promoting this idea (first suggested by the Polish astronomer Copernicus in 1543), and was forced to repudiate his beliefs and writings on the subject.

The point is, of course, that until Copernicus and Galileo began to sow seeds of doubt about the way things were with the Sun and the Earth, everybody *knew* that the Earth was the centre of everything. It was what they were taught, an absolute fact. But those seeds of doubt led to enlightenment, and that is what this book can do for you – sow seeds of doubt about what you know of yourself, which will eventually lead to enlightenment and subsequent empowerment.

The clue to the real you and your true potential lies with your ancestors. Not your recent ancestors, your parents and grandparents; not even *their* parents or even their parents' parents... but your distant ancestors of tens of thousands of years ago. Those people gave you an inheritance you deserve, an inheritance of success.

In the Beginning...

One hundred thousand years ago, the human race lived in groups of twenty-five to fifty individuals, hunting and gathering their food from the land. They were already a developed race, having probably been around for some three hundred thousand years at least, but these were the first of the race that looked like us, and, in a primitive way, behaved like us. For thousands of years, their way of life scarcely changed. Instincts and response patterns were handed on from generation to generation in what amounted to a genetically pure chain. These humans would have had no qualms about incest or inbreeding, because those concepts simply would not have entered the realms of thought.

3

There would obviously have been aggressive tribes and peaceful tribes; and because their way of life was constant, the skills needed to deal with that way of life became inborn and instinctive, so that successive generations became steadily more adapted to the environment in which they lived.

Tens of thousand of years passed… something like *fifty times* the amount of time that has elapsed since the days of Jesus Christ and the Roman Empire. Then, something of extreme importance happened, something that was to affect the whole of the human race for ever more. Something that was to affect *you*.

The first settlements were formed.

A Golden Opportunity

It does not sound particularly important, but the effect on the wandering tribes was dramatic and polarising. For the peace-loving tribes it would have been an ideal situation; no need any more to wander the land in search of food – simply farm your own crops and livestock and share the work within the community. Instead of fighting the land, adapt to it and tame it, and use its resources for survival and comfort. These tribes became the Settlers and discovered their evolutionary destiny.

For others, those who had always simply taken whatever they wanted, this presented a golden opportunity of a different sort. They could wait until a settlement was formed and everything was nicely under control, then simply move in and take over. Any of the original occupants who protested too much could be either killed or kicked out, and the rest, observing this, would simply continue to maintain the place for the benefit of the newcomers. These Warrior types now had something really worth fighting for, and some of them took over several settlements and controlled quite large areas of land as a result.

For yet others, all this would be too much. They had never had the stomach for fighting, nor any wish to do loads of hard work for the benefit of somebody else. And now they had no desire whatsoever to stand around getting caught up in the crossfire between the

Settlers and a bunch of club-wielding roughnecks wearing strings of animal teeth around their necks. So they retained the instinctive Nomadic urges of their earliest forefathers – keep on the move, do not get involved, and constantly look for someplace new and interesting. They also eventually developed skills like thieving, bartering and entertaining, since this was an effective way to earn their keep 'on the road'.

Civilisation

This was the origin of what we now know as Civilisation, and our inheritance is the in-built instincts of those early people. There has been much interbreeding ever since and there are no longer any pure specimens of any one tribe. But there were some ninety thousand years *at least* of wandering savage, against relatively few years of civilisation, and evolution moves very slowly indeed. The original instincts still run high.

We each carry, as our parents did and their parents and grandparents before them, the genes from each of those three major tribes of mankind; but one set will usually be dominant, giving rise to a behaviour pattern that governs how we are, where and how we will be successful, the way we conduct our lives… or would, if our way of being were not 'modified' by our early experiences. Because, since genetic selection appears to be a random process, so that, for example, Settler parents can produce Nomad children, *it is entirely possible that you were brought up by parents or others who have a completely different set of instinctive traits.* This is important, for it would obviously have a clouding effect upon your real personality, upon what is inherently right for you, diluting your inherited strengths and attributes.

Just imagine, for a moment, the implications of this. Let us assume that you have inherited a dominant set of Warrior genes, but both your parents are Settlers. They will try to teach you to be tolerant of others and adapt to situations, to 'go with the flow' and roll with the punches. They might even suggest that you attempt to make friends of your adversaries and always try to see others' points of view. They will, perhaps, teach you that you should always give others the benefit of the doubt.

5

*But all of your subconscious instincts insist that you should be dealing with life in a forthright, 'hands-on' and extremely **direct** manner! That you should be leading, not following; giving the orders, not taking them.*

Under those circumstances, there would be a continual conflict in the subconscious that might well lead to all sorts of frustrations and complexes. It certainly would not be conducive to success. Even if you eventually managed to override that 'programming', you still might not be able to fully enjoy any success you found, because of an underlying feeling that you had achieved your aims in a way that was somehow not quite right, that did not match what you had been taught was the 'proper' way to do things.

We have all come across families in which a child appears to be totally different from his/her parents, or brothers and sisters. The parents will perhaps say things like, "He probably takes after his great-grandfather..." Well, maybe that child *has* inherited the same set of dominant genes that powered his great-grandfather, but they would have powered a whole host of far more ancient ancestors first!

It works something like this. Assume that:

> *Parent A is 50% Warrior, 35% Settler, 15% Nomad.*
> *Parent B is 50% Nomad, 35% Settler, 15% Warrior.*

If they have three children, it is very likely that at least one of them will inherit the set of genes which, added together, is more dominant than either of their own major traits. It is a simple illustration and not technically very accurate, but it serves to show how easily the phenomenon of having the 'wrong' parents can come about.

Three Tribes

Warriors, Settlers and Nomads, the three main tribes of man. Discover which you are related to and you could be on the way to greater success and greater enjoyment of life generally. In this book, you will have the opportunity to do just that; more than that, you will also discover how to tap into the subconscious processes of *each* of the groups in your mind, allowing you to adopt the responses and reactions of whichever one of them best suits any situation in which you find yourself.

There could surely be no better tool for success, whatever success means to you, than to be able to match yourself equally to any or all of life's situations!

The Warrior

Let's have a look at what these ancient ancestors of ours might have been like, beginning with the Warriors.

Obviously the Warrior tribes would have been physically powerful, but there was more to these people than brute force. The best amongst them became expert planners who prepared for every possibility, quick and perceptive thinkers who could foresee every pitfall and every danger to their plans and schemes. Their need to control and conquer others meant that they had little or no time for compassion or emotion; there was no room for compassion if you wanted to come out tops on the battlefield. In fact they would have been capable of being totally ruthless, completely unconcerned about the feelings of others. Self was what mattered, and what self wanted.

Sensitivity was not in the frame for these people, nor were any 'airy-fairy' ideas. No-nonsense practicalities were what they needed – tools, plans, methods, foolproof strategies. A means to an end, and as quick and straight forward as possible. In the earliest days, they were true savages, but savages with a shrewd intelligence, who could be devious and manipulative when necessary.

Of course, modern Warriors do not usually make their living by going around killing people and fighting battles and wars... or do they? They may not kill people in the physical sense, but perhaps they do so metaphorically in the business world, via take-overs, mergers and redundancies. And did you ever hear that expression 'Making a killing' applied to business? There can be a great deal of devious behaviour in the business world, as well as tussles for control in all sorts of other situations, including the home.

7

Modern Warriors certainly share one particular aspect of behaviour with their ancestors, an aspect that has hardly changed at all over the centuries. Their major ancestral memory is the need to be in control, and they always possess the modern skills and traits associated with that drive – ready aggression, the ability and desire to manipulate others when necessary, a speed of thought that is second to none, and the desire to take charge. They are also usually very logical.

At a higher level they may well be generals in an army, perhaps 'captains of industry' or high-flying executives, high-ranking police officers or senior computer programmers. At the other end of the scale, where inner resources may not be recognised or used properly, we find inspectors/investigators of various sorts, traffic wardens, and security guards. Individuals from the other groups may do those jobs, too, of course, but the Warrior type excels at them and *enjoys* excelling at them. Do not be misled into thinking that this is necessarily an unpleasant group of people; they are usually no more so than individuals in the other groups might be, because their more extreme Warrior characteristics have been 'watered down' by the influence of the other groups. It is true, though, that their direct manner can sometimes be intimidating, and they are not usually thought of as 'nice' people – but they are usually unconcerned about the opinions of others, anyway.

The Settler

Settler types were totally different. These were peace-loving people who wanted nothing more than to be left to themselves to tend their land and rear their families to help them continue their calm existence. They were community-minded, recognising the worth of sharing tasks and keeping harmony within their group, so they developed an understanding of others and a high degree of tolerance to the differing opinions of those who shared their space. They were also adaptable and resourceful, using whatever nature provided them with to survive, and would use aggression only as a last resort, in defence.

It is impossible to hurry the forces of nature, and understanding this led to a patient approach to life and living, with an ability to tolerate discomfort in the knowledge that there were better times ahead. Settlers were optimists who enjoyed what was without hankering too much after what might have been.

Modern-day Settlers do not have to be farmers or raisers of live-stock, though some of them actually are. They can frequently be found in the caring/nurturing professions, or wherever tact and diplomacy or any sort of communication skills are needed. Their major ancestral memories are of adaptability and problem-solving, and at a high level they can be successful writers, leading therapists or doctors, or experts on animal care and husbandry; at the lower levels, they may be care attendants for the elderly or very young, gardeners, or home-builders. Their adaptability can cause them to sometimes seem weak-willed, but they all have a resilience that can put the other two groups to shame.

Generally speaking, these are the nice people of the world–respon-sive, communicative, and usually interested in the welfare of others. They are usually ready to lend a hand when it is needed, and tend to have a cheerful and optimistic outlook most of the time. But they can become quite despondent when things go wrong, a throwback, no doubt, to the days when crop failures or dead or stolen animals heralded hard and unpleasant times ahead. These people are not 'quitters'; they will stick with a problem or situation until it is either resolved or finished.

The Nomad

The Nomads were following the very earliest instincts of the species. The whole race had been nomadic originally and when the first settlements were being formed, these individuals pre-ferred to remain that way – not for them the emotional attachments that the Settlers formed, or the hard work and frequent disap-pointment involved in taming the land. Not for them, either, the meticulous planning of the Warrior. They did not want the risks of battle, or the necessity to be constantly on guard lest those whom you had vanquished should suddenly rise up against you.

Whereas the Warriors and Settlers were always in large groups, the Nomads would have travelled in much smaller bands, even sometimes as individuals. They would have been light-hearted people with little or no need to put down roots. They enjoyed wandering from one place to another, leaving behind any problems or difficulties that might accrue wherever they stopped for a while. Eventually they became wandering minstrels, entertainers, tinkers and the like, always difficult to pin down, never staying in one guise or situation long enough to be saddled with responsibility. Relying on their wits to survive, they were probably far more independent and charismatic than the other two groups put together.

Modern Nomads do not necessarily wander far and wide, although some will be sailors or long-distance lorry drivers. Most of them, though, manage to control that inherent wanderlust, as well as the aversion to responsibility, but they all have an in-built urge to be extremely individual, not to be part of the common herd. They need change, drama and excitement, and because they enjoy feelings of importance, they often spend considerable time attempting to be the centre of attention. Nomads, always charismatic, are frequently the 'larger-than-life' characters who can be quite 'showy' in their demeanour.

Not uncommonly, Nomads can have difficulties in relationships, since they are inclined to be more interested in themselves than they are in others. They are often clever and witty, frequently 'ideas people' with original and innovative plans and schemes, always with an eye to creating an impression.

At a high level, they are found amongst the ranks of actors, barristers, and financial experts; at lower levels, they might be minor entertainers, salesmen or company representatives – or even con men!

The Real Truth

The next chapter will help you discover just who *your* ancestors were. It will also provide a detailed character assessment along with a breakdown of your inherited strengths and weaknesses, and suggestions for how to use them or overcome them.

Of course, you may already feel that you have already recognised yourself in the preceding 'snapshots', but don't jump to any conclusions just yet. Many of us are as we are only because we believe that is how we are supposed to be – after all, that is what we have been taught since birth. But our beliefs can so easily be wrong.

Read on to find out the real truth!

Chapter Two
Who Do You Think You Are?

In this chapter, you will discover your *true* ancestry – not who your aunts, uncles and cousins are or were, but your origins of thousands of years ago, your true birthright.

You are about to find out which is your major 'tribe', and how much of each of the others you carry within you. All you have to do is answer a dozen questions, but you must answer them with TOTAL honesty. There are no right or wrong answers, and no better or best answer to any question; the questions are not designed to test how good you are, but to reveal who your ancestors were and what characteristics you are likely to have inherited. If you try to make your answers fit what you think you *should* be saying, rather than what is actually the truth, then you will not discover your true self at all, only what you believe you should be – and it may well turn out that you have spent your life trying to be someone whose characteristics don't suit you at all! When you discover your *true* self, you discover your *true* strengths.

Think carefully about each question before you answer – take all the time you need, because speed is not a factor here.

Mark each question on a scale of 1–10. Alternate questions are 'double edged', looking at related but different sides of your nature.

Make a note of your answers – you'll need them in a later chapter.

1. **How** determined/dogmatic are you?   7

2. **How** easily can you 'speak your mind'?   6

3. **How** shrewd/cynical are you?   6

4. **How** argumentative can you be?   7

    TOTAL   26 $(\div\ by\ T=$ 37 $)$

5. **How** adaptable/indecisive can you be?   6

6. **How** important is it for you to be liked?   7

7. **How** reliable/over-trusting can you be?   6

8. **How** easygoing are you?   4

    TOTAL   23 $(\div\ by\ T=$ 33 $)$

9. **How** inspiring/over-dramatic can you be?   4

10. **How** easily can you shrug off or

     ignore criticism?   4

11. **How** spontaneous/impulsive can you be?   5

12. **How** impatient can you be?   7

    TOTAL   20 $(\div\ by\ T=$ 14 $)$

FINAL TOTAL | 69 |

$\div$ *by 100*   0.69 $=T$

14

The first group of questions (1–4) assesses Warrior potentials; the second looks at the Settler traits; and the third is concerned with the Nomadic personality. Add the scores of each group together, giving three totals. Add them together and divide that total by 100, calling the answer 'T'. By dividing the total of each group in turn by T, you will find the percentage of each group in any one individual.

What Does it All Mean?

Now you have discovered your true self, you may have had something of a surprise – many people do! You may even feel that you want to dispute the result. However, it is unlikely to be wrong, especially if there is more than about 5% difference between the two highest percentages. Where there is less than this, you will probably find yourself exhibiting fairly even amounts of each group; in these circumstances, you should pay particular attention to the 'Influence of other groups' heading in each section below. A few individuals discover all three scores to be remarkably even, which indicates a multifaceted personality. These lucky people are able to turn their mind to just about anything they wish and can usually find whatever resources they need. Most of them will not be bothering to read this book!

Now we will have a detailed look at a complete assessment of your personality as indicated by the test, including your strengths and weaknesses, your attitude to your fellow human beings, even the sort of career where you are most likely to find success. Of course, social status, background, family values and other incidental factors tend to govern how the personality is used or expressed. For instance, the negative Nomad from a poor family may seem to be a flashy and 'cheap' show-off, while a similar personality with a wealthy background may well exhibit the same shallow tendencies but use very expensive 'props' to do so. Though the two may look startlingly different, they will be essentially similar – there will be no real substance to back up the repeated claims of importance, no real charisma.

The Settler

Personality Profile:

Sociable: Gets on well with almost anybody.

Intuitive: A high level of instinct and general awareness.

Adaptable: Able to make the best of any situation.

Achilles heel: The need to be liked.

Evidence of this personality begins to show in the earliest years of life, between birth and about two and a half years old. At around this time, the child discovers that sensing Mother's mood and responding accordingly produces a pleasant and satisfying degree of attention. The Settler child soon learns that the same is true in the world at large: even when the environment seems cold and unwelcoming, by adapting behaviour patterns to conform with what others seem to want, the child can get lots of positive attention. Every individual is subject to this understanding and knowledge-based phase of development, but only where it exactly fits the birth predisposition, the inherited ancestral memory, will these personality traits continue to dominate.

The Settler personality, being able to fit in with almost any situation, is necessarily a kind of psychological chameleon. The most obvious traits are a pleasant and responsive attitude to others but, interestingly, they do sometimes have a tendency towards mood swings, changing from happy to miserable – or the other way round – at the slightest provocation, the smallest event. Another trait that can catch others unaware is a marked tendency to an 'all or nothing' response on occasions, in which if they cannot have *absolutely* what they want, they will simply refuse to have any part of it at all and will 'cut off their nose to spite their face'. This is usually noticeable when they are unhappy about something but are too nice to say so outright. However, as excellent talkers and communicators, Settlers are unrivalled when it comes to having an instinctive grasp of all that is going on around them. They are usually reliable and come over as 'nice' people, which they usually are.

16

Influence of the Other Groups
(Only applicable where there is a score of 25% or more):

Where there is enough influence it is more than likely that there will be evidence of the *control, determination* and *cynicism* that are the predominating features of the Warrior personality. Settlers will tend to use these qualities rather subtly, applying their instinctive grasp of other people's thought processes to gain control (often by a well-placed, devastatingly undermining comment) and maybe employing the determination inwardly, developing astonishingly high levels of self-discipline. Any cynicism will tend to be focused around the idea that others are inclined to take advantage of them or in some way 'pull the wool over their eyes'.

When the enthusiastic, uninhibited, irresponsible tendencies of the Nomadic personality come into play here the first two traits tend to reinforce the natural optimism inherent in the Settler individual, while the irresponsibility can sometimes produce an out-of-character display of unreliability under certain circumstances. These circumstances vary from one individual to another but are more often than not the result of pique: "You've made me feel so bad that I simply can't go into work today" is a good example.

Physical Traits

Settlers are easy to recognise from their physiology. They are responsive during conversation, with active but not excessive body and head movements: they nod and smile when they should, and express any disagreement politely and tactfully. Their facial expressions are reactive to the conversation, and they tend to smile often, unless they are depressed. Any tension or anxiety tends to speed up body movements and speech, and makes any lines on the face more visible, causing the expression to become more worried or anxious.

Positive Attributes

◆   Instinctive understanding of others.
◆   Caring and compassionate.

◆   Unequalled communication skills.
◆   Persuasive and naturally diplomatic.
◆   Learns from errors – own *and* other people's.
◆   Generally optimistic, cheerful and polite.
◆   Confident and easygoing.
◆   Builds and uses a sound and wide-ranging knowledge base.
◆   Tolerant: can see the best in people and get the best out of them.
◆   Powerful instinctive responses: can seem to possess a genuine sixth sense about other people's hidden attitudes or mood shifts.
◆   Flexible approach to others' plans.
◆   Can turn a setback into an advantage.
◆   Can adjust easily to any environment as necessary.
◆   Can easily 'ride' disappointments or failures while maintaining optimism and self-belief: a natural survivor

Particular strengths: Communication, teaching, writing, diplomacy, troubleshooting, counselling, negotiating, marketing, caring... anything where an understanding of people and their needs and motivation is of paramount importance. Success can be found not only by *doing* but by being *involved* in these fields, either directly or indirectly.

Negative Attributes

Many Settler individuals appear to show none – or very few – of the following traits. **They are only tendencies and not necessarily present.**

The complexity of the Settler personality can be exasperating to others if the individual slides into a negative behavioural mode. Negative Settlers can be just on the brink of success when they will suddenly give up, claiming that they simply have not got what it takes, even if other people think they have. Feelings of inferiority and inadequacy can lead to problems with decision-making and displays of underconfidence or unassertiveness. They can also seem to take far too much notice of the opinions of others, with an excessive need to be liked sometimes leading to difficulty in saying 'No' when necessary. There is often a dismal failure to recognise the value or level of their own attributes and skills – feelings of failure or of being in some way fraudulent are often evident. They are prone to shyness, depression and/or bouts of debilitating melancholia. These negative traits may very well be born out of the ancestral memories of oppression by Warriors and desertion by Nomads.

Limitations: Because of their adaptable nature, there are not very many things the Settler cannot turn to. There are, though, specific weaknesses with: control (corporate or individual), discipline, planning and organisation. Impersonal situations (that is, situations in which there is not some sort of human connection or involvement) should be avoided if possible.

The positively biased Settler personality is able to use communicative skills, intuition and knowledge to become highly effective and influential, often making a success out of helping others to become successful. Those who allow the weak negative traits to dominate are in danger of ending up dejected and ineffective with a feeling that 'it wasn't fair'. The greatest chances of success are found where there is no real need to be assertive, authoritarian, or determinedly in control.

The Warrior

Personality Profile:

Forceful: Can always make their presence felt.

Resolute: High levels of tenacity and determination.

Organisational: Able to plan well and bring those plans to fruition.

Achilles heel: The need to always be in control.

This personality generally starts to become apparent between the ages of two and five years old, when the child is learning self control, seeking to gain mastery over words, body and environment – with varying degrees of success. The child discovers that being determined or stubborn produces a gratifying result and that certain eventualities can be predicted and therefore planned for. To a child born with a Warrior predisposition, the sense of being **in control** is more rewarding than the earlier Settler phase of discovering communicative interaction with others. It is, in fact, satisfying to the point where it 'feels right', and sets the seal on this individual's behaviour patterns for life.

Warriors tend to have a reputation for firmness and a no-nonsense attitude to life. Psychologically stronger than either the Settler or Nomad personality types, they find no difficulty in taking charge of things, and they easily win the respect of others. They are cautious yet quick thinkers who are unsurpassed at finding and exploiting the flaw in any argument. On the negative side, there can sometimes be a problem with cynicism and jealousy, and there is not the immediately friendly response generally found in the Settler. Indeed, when a question is put to a warrior, there will sometimes be a significant pause before they answer, and the answer will often be carefully phrased in such a way to leave as many options open as possible.

Influence of the Other Groups
(Only applicable where there is a 'score' of 25% or more)

Where either of the other groups has sufficient influence it is possible that their major characteristics will show themselves from time to time. This is only *possible*, though, because the very direct and forthright nature of the Warrior's own traits tends to overpower the more subtle Settler qualities, and to stifle what they may view as lack of control in the Nomadic individual.

Of the two, however, it is the Nomad influence that is most likely to be noticeable, especially during an argument or confrontation. In such circumstances the Warrior/Nomad may become very loud, *uninhibitedly* vindictive, and occasionally violent. At other times the *enthusiasm* may be channelled into planning; there can then be an obsessive need to pursue a plan or idea that may not be totally sound – the 'bee in the bonnet' effect. The Warrior/Nomad combination is not a particularly happy one either, for the individual or the people around him or her.

Where Settler traits are in evidence, the apparent *sociability* may well be double-edged: the individual may watch for opportunities or information that may later be of use on in some way. Any *persuasiveness* tends to show itself as a tendency for this individual to nag or harangue; similarly, there may be *changeable* moods as with the Settler personality, but in the Warrior/Settler the mood swings will be darker or more violent.

Physical Traits

The Warrior is the least physically animated of the three groups. There are few changes of facial expression during conversation, and few changes of body position. The angle of the head, in particular, may remain unchanged for longish periods, making the Warrior's look a bit like a skilled card player, who gives away absolutely nothing about his or her inner thought processes. Warriors appear to be – and indeed are – watchful and perceptive, with a steady gaze that may turn away from their conversation partner if they are nervous. Any tension or anxiety will show in a taut body shape and a set facial expression leaning towards irritability or hostility.

Positive Attributes

♦ Determined and tenacious; goal-oriented.
♦ Unsurpassed organisational abilities.
♦ Excellent planner, both short- and long-term.
♦ Calm and unruffled in emergencies.
♦ Energetic, independent and self-sufficient.
♦ Perceptive and easily able to spot the pitfalls in a plan or situation.
♦ Sound but not necessarily fast decision-making abilities.
♦ Security-conscious and naturally discreet.
♦ Natural team leader and coordinator.
♦ Quick thinker in discussion or argument, able to easily see and exploit loopholes or advantages.
♦ Methodical approach to planning and follow-up.
♦ Organised approach to problem-solving.
♦ Practical and logical.
♦ Good at recalling and using facts and figures.

Particular strengths: control, leadership, planning and organisation, perception/detection, security, discipline, accounting, science and technology, information-handling, practicalities, enforcement. Many barristers, other legal personnel, politicians, and 'captains of industry' are Warrior personalities.

Negative Attributes

As with the other two groups, these traits are only possible tendencies and are not necessarily evident in any one individual – indeed, it is unlikely that any one individual will show all these traits. Among the Warrior's positive traits are a decisive and direct nature, and this forthright attitude also tends to be reflected in the negative traits.

The Warrior character is inclined to force rather than subtlety and in negative mode is usually pedantic, domineering and impatient, and can appear rude and sarcastic. Warriors have a driving need to be in control and can sometimes be quite ruthless in their determination to be so, as they are very good at manipulating people and events to their advantage – this, of course, may be viewed as positive trait under some circumstances.

The two things Warriors hate most are not getting their own way, and having to admit that they are wrong. Underneath all their attempts to maintain power and control, there are often secret feelings of self-doubt, leading to cynicism and jealousy. They are prone to phobia, hypochondria and/or obsessive thought or behaviour patterns. Sometimes they may actually take a considerable amount of pleasure in being bad-tempered or unreasonable.

Limitations: Not good at taking orders, diplomacy, intuitive work, negotiation, or situations requiring tolerance or patience with others.

The positively biased Warrior character can easily rise to the top of the success ladder in many forms of business, commerce and industry; those who do not succeed in overcoming the considerable ferocity of their negative traits can end up totally unsuccessful, friendless and bitter. The greatest chances of success will be found in fields where the individual is able to be in full and direct control of just about anything.

The Nomad

Personality Profile:

Restless: Must always have something going on.

Charismatic: Naturally outgoing.

Evidential: 'What you see is what you get.'

Achilles Heel: The need for constant stimulation.

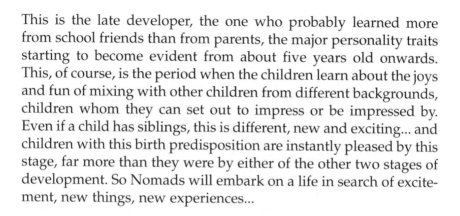

This is the late developer, the one who probably learned more from school friends than from parents, the major personality traits starting to become evident from about five years old onwards. This, of course, is the period when the children learn about the joys and fun of mixing with other children from different backgrounds, children whom they can set out to impress or be impressed by. Even if a child has siblings, this is different, new and exciting... and children with this birth predisposition are instantly pleased by this stage, far more than they were by either of the other two stages of development. So Nomads will embark on a life in search of excitement, new things, new experiences...

The Nomadic personality in its purest form tends towards extremes in many things. Nomads enjoy life to the full and can give much pleasure to a great many people along the way – except for the occasions when they get carried away with frivolity and excitement. These are the times when they love to shock others with loud and embarrassing behaviour, and act amazed when someone complains about their excesses. This exuberance tends to show itself quite often and can be quite exhausting and tiresome for their companions. Most of the time, though, this personality is tempered by more sensible traits from the other two groups, often resulting in an individual who can uplift others with their irrepressible sense of fun and enthusiasm.

Influence of the Other Groups
(Only applicable with a 'score' of 25% or more)

Nomads really *need* an offsetting influence to be able to cope with the more boring and mundane aspects of living, and of earning a living. Fortunately, the Nomadic character, whilst often noisy, tends to easily absorb such influences. This is especially true, of course, where its own percentage is not particularly dominant.

The most likely group to make its effects felt is the Warrior, probably because of its lack of complexity. The result is sometimes an inspiring combination of flamboyance and industry, capable of surprisingly good and reliable work with quite serious matters – as long as the individual is allowed to be innovative in some way. Financial, utilitarian and legal areas seem to be particularly favoured.

Less comfortable is the combination with the Settler personality, because of the conflict between patience and the need for instant gratification. The *sociable* outlook of the Settler then combines with the natural enthusiasm and exuberance of the Nomad and can produce a back-slapping, laugh-a-minute individual. The *changeability* is revealed as a tendency to pout and suddenly and noisily 'throw a wobbly' when things aren't to the person's liking. When it shows, *persuasiveness* will often manifest itself as a continual 'whinge' or grumble about some restriction, imagined or exaggerated, that has been placed upon the individual. Without the modifying influence of the Warrior group, this combination can sometimes seem annoyingly childish.

Physical Traits

Animated behaviour is the most obvious trait here but, as with most things in this group, it tends to be exaggerated. There are excessive movements of the head and face, the body, and especially the hands. Nomads can liven up any gathering with sparkling wit – as long as not too much serious stuff is expected from them. Often quite generous and outgoing, and almost exclusively extroverts, Nomads are always on the lookout for something new and exciting to do. They adore telling jokes and stories with lots of noise and action, and they always do it well. Under any sort of pressure, they tend to become louder and more expansive in their gestures and movements.

Positive Attributes

◆   Enthusiasm for new projects.
◆   Lively and alert approach to life and work.
◆   Inspirational in outlook and communication.
◆   Unsurpassable in publicity and promotion matters.
◆   Exceptionally confident and outgoing.
◆   Uninhibited in all areas of life.
◆   Sharp eye for creating an image.
◆   Skilled at finding novel and ingenious solutions to problems.
◆   Uncomplicated personality – what you see is what you get.
◆   Exceptional presentation skills.
◆   Ready wit, especially in response to others.
◆   Natural ability to entertain and amuse others.
◆   Natural ability to inspire and uplift others.

Particular strengths: presentation, promotional situations, direct sales, entertainment, new or novel products or schemes... anything where image, persona and/or enthusiasm are important. Many actors and 'super-salespersons' have a predominantly Nomadic personality. Because the deeper human emotional values are a total mystery to them, they often choose to work in the worlds of finance or law, which are just about as far removed from the world of emotions as it is possible to be.

Negative Attributes

As with the Settler and Warrior personalities, these negative traits will not necessarily be apparent.

The biggest problem for Nomads is maintaining application of effort, and as a result they can appear unreliable or fickle. They themselves are unconcerned about this, however, relying on sheer force of personality and charisma to see them through, and usually getting away with it; they may even boast about it. There is a childish need for instant gratification – they cannot abide waiting for things to happen – and a distinct tendency to flamboyantly exaggerate their successes. Their relationships are usually distinctly one-sided, and they are masters of tactlessness and bad taste. Under pressure, they are prone to dramatic illnesses like paralysis, apparent blindness, 'blackouts', memory loss, etc., which may or may not be genuine.

Limitations: Not usually very good at routine or mundane matters, methodical planning, self-discipline, minutiae or anything that needs patience or sustained concentration... *but* see 'Influence of the other groups', above.

The positive Nomadic personality can be successful at anything where an outgoing personality and true charisma are needed. Nomads have trouble if things become in any way 'heavy', and may revert to negativity and noisiness very quickly. The greatest chances for success are found where the natural flamboyance of the type does not need to be restricted.

In the next chapter, we will use the remnants of your ancestral memories to develop physical images of your ancestry, images that will help you to sharply focus your inner resources.

Quick Recognition Guide

Here is a quick recognition guide for each group which, while it is not as accurate as the questionnaire, will give you a good idea of where anybody 'fits', just by watching them for a moment or two. Learn the characteristics, behaviour patterns and reactions of each personality type, and you will never look at people in quite the same way again!

 Settler

Physiology:	Responsive body and head movements. Frequent smiles.
Positive:	Caring, cheerful, pleasant, talkative and tolerant. 'People' people.
Negative:	Depressive, indecisive, underconfident. Prone to mood swings.

 **Warrior**

Physiology:	Fairly straight-faced, few body response patterns, steady gaze.
Positive:	Practical, tenacious and self-sufficient. Quick thinkers.
Negative:	Suspicious, dictatorial, manipulative. Cannot easily admit mistakes.

 Nomad

Physiology:	Often expansive in gestures. Can be animated and noisy. Laughs easily.
Positive:	Fun-loving, enthusiastic, outgoing. Inspiring and optimistic.
Negative:	Unreliable, childish, boastful. Prone to exaggerating minor successes.

Chapter Three
Looking Back

It's best to read this chapter when you have nothing particularly pressing to deal with – you will need to be able to concentrate, and to allow your imagination free rein without distractions or time constraints. Also, it's a good idea to read the entire chapter through before attempting to do the exercises, allowing yourself to give deep thought where you need to.

In this chapter, we are going to delve into the depths of your subconscious mind to discover the images that you already carry there of your three ancestral types. You might want to conduct the search for each of them on separate days, since it is easy to lose focus and concentration if you try to do it all at once.

We are not, of course, going to find a physical likeness of three of your actual relatives from thousands of years ago! What we are going to do is discover the *archetypal images* of your ancestors – the images that, in your subconscious mind, actually personify the Warrior, the Settler and the Nomad. Linked to these images, even though you may not yet be aware of it, is an understanding of and a 'feel' for the behaviour patterns and resources of the types; they are your link to your deepest and most established instincts, instincts for survival and success that have been evolving since the dawning of the human race.

The easiest one to find will be that of your major personality group; the other two may be less easy, but you do need to find them, so do not be tempted to skip one or the other. You will soon learn how to use these archetypes to achieve your goals and enhance your life.

It is not at all necessary to match your sex – it is quite possible for a female to have a male archetype and *vice versa*. For instance, a female might see her Warrior as an armoured knight on horseback, or a male might perceive his as a Boadicea or an Amazonian type. The only important thing is that your archetypes are a product of *your* imagination; seeking help from friends or family will produce *their* archetypes, who may be of no use to you at all.

It is very likely that, when you have finished, you will realise that one or more of the archetypes you have developed is completely different from the way you perceive yourself. *This is evidence that you are not using all your resources in a way that suits your instinctive drives. The archetype that you have discovered will allow you to discover your* true *'inner self'!* It is a psychological fact that your subconscious cannot actually invent anything – all it can do is draw upon what knowledge you already have, your experiences and your instincts. Anything you imagine is based upon a reality somewhere in your mind, even if you are not consciously aware of that reality. Anything your mind produces is a product of how your mind works.

Before we begin the search, here is a simple concentration enhancer that produces a beautifully relaxed state in which thoughts can flow easily and steadily through your mind. It takes only a few minutes and doubles as a superb stress-relief routine that you can use whenever you need it. It's a good idea to learn how to do this before progressing to the search for your archetypes.

Concentration Enhancer

Make sure you are sitting quite comfortably – some people actually find a straight-backed chair better than an armchair. Have both your feet flat on the floor and let your hands lie loose in your lap. Close your eyes, and imagine every single muscle in your body to be completely relaxed. If you have difficulty relaxing, just imagine just how it would feel if you were relaxed. Now start to steady your breathing, gradually slowing it until you are breathing so slowly and so gently, so steadily and evenly, that you almost would not disturb even a single strand of a feather placed in front of your nostrils. Don't rush... you cannot hurry relaxation. After a little while, you will feel yourself becoming stiller and quieter, and your senses may seem to become more alert. You could find your mind becoming as calm as your body, or you might feel as if it is more alert than ever before. Either way, you are ready.

If you find it difficult to become fully relaxed via this simple method, there is a more detailed – and more lengthy – relaxation routine later on in the book.

The Search

If you believe that you cannot see images in your mind's eye, it is a good idea to read Appendix One before going any further. This will help you to become proficient at this essential skill.

We will start with the Warrior. What does the term 'Warrior' suggest to you? Maybe you find yourself thinking of a prehistoric individual whose major attribute was physical endurance and strength, a Crusader from the Middle Ages, or something entirely different. If it is an image of someone you know, just reject it – it is not what you are looking for or what you need to find. It does not matter, though, if you realise that you are thinking of a character you have seen in a film, or read about in a book. The reason that this particular character caught your imagination in the first place is precisely because it fits in with your ancestral memories. Don't work too hard at it at this stage – it is enough just to let your mind dwell for a moment or two on the concept of the Warrior.

Here are some Warrior archetypes – not an exhaustive list by any means, nor in any particular order: Celtic Kings and Chieftains, Warrior Queens, Normans, Vikings, Crusaders, Knights, Native Americans, Samurai, Zulus, Shoguns, Trojans, Nubian Kings and Queens, Roman Gladiators and Centurions, Chinese and Japanese Emperors, Ancient Huns, Saxons, Gurkhas.

You will notice the absence of modern-day military warriors. They are a little recent to be used as archetypes, since they were developed from archetypes themselves. Nonetheless, if that is what you find, go with it.

When you find the archetype that is going to work for you, it will 'feel' right. You will be able to see an image in your mind's eye – you may envision specific features, and perhaps even have an idea as to how this individual actually is. Of course, it is your imagination that will do this, because imagination is just about the only true conscious link that we have with our subconscious. When it feels right, it is because it matches our ancestral memories and therefore suits our instincts.

Perhaps you will visualise an inscrutable Oriental with a colourful costume and mystic skills. Perhaps it will be a foot soldier of the Roman legions or a King of some long-forgotten tribe, ruling his cohorts with an iron hand. Perhaps it is a stealthy hunter who is neither seen nor heard until it is too late. The image does not need to be historically accurate – that would only be somebody else's interpretation, anyway – or based on any facts. What it does need to be is *vivid* in your mind.

Make it Real

Now it is time to use the concentration routine outlined above; once you are ready, allow your imagination either to work on the image you already have, or to produce one for you to work on.

See this individual in your mind moving about, rather than as a still photograph – fighting, pursuing a foe, eating and drinking… even making love, if that is what comes to mind. Give that powerful imagination of yours full rein. Imagine yourself to be back in time with this individual: imagine that you can hear them, feel their body warmth and maybe skin texture, actually *smell* their presence. Even give the person a name, if you wish. This technique can be very powerful, and it is the way that many writers create their characters.

When you have what might be viewed as a working model, it is time to move on to the next archetype. Once you have formed your three archetypes in this way, we will go on to a second and more detailed stage of development.

In Search of the Settler

Now you have your Warrior available to your thoughts, we will seek the far gentler Settler archetype. You might have already formed an opinion of these people while reading about them in

Chapter 1, and may have become aware that they are far more complex characters, though less dramatic, than either the Warriors or the Nomads. As a result, it can be a little more difficult to find what you are looking for – unless it is your major group.

Here are a few Settler archetypes: Homesteaders, Ancient Farmers, Livestock Workers, Ancient Builders, Carers of all descriptions, Healers, Craftspeople of all types, Teachers, Monks, Nuns, Prophets and Seers, Tailors and Dressmakers, Barbers, Shopkeepers, Researchers, Philosophers, Artists, Musicians, Composers, and 'Searchers for Truth'.

Again, allow images just to drift through your mind at first; don't try to force anything or drag something forward. Maybe there will be a vague image that you cannot quite focus on; it will become clear soon enough if you let it, but it will stay stubbornly vague if you try to force the issue. It can often be easier to find the image of the Settler by 'feel' rather than by a visual impression. You might find yourself capturing a sense of a wonderfully at ease, peaceful individual; or you may feel the enjoyment of the simplicity of life on the land, or perhaps the satisfaction of teaching, passing on knowledge. Or you may get a sense of the pleasure of producing a work of art or a piece of fine furniture.

Whatever you find, this is going to be a character who is in touch with his or her emotions and is not ashamed of them. Settler men can be gentle and kind. Settler women can be angry. Either one can rage against any form of injustice, and either one can forgive another their transgressions and let bygones be bygones.

Now do the same exercise as with the Warrior, using the relaxation routine and then allowing your imagination to do the rest. You don't need to make notes or write anything down, because if you have found the right image it will stay in your mind just as certainly and clearly as if you had known this person for years. Or for thousands of years... The Settler is a multifaceted and more complicated personality than either of the others, and you might need to explore this archetype for longer than that of the Warrior or the Nomad. Of course, if you are a Settler type yourself, your understanding will be faster. If you are a Warrior type, you may find it difficult, at first, to accept this more peaceful side of your nature.

Chasing the Nomad

The Nomad part of your character is the colourful part, the part that likes to be the centre of attention and knows how to get there. Nomads are inclined towards dramatic displays – especially if anything goes wrong – and love to be different from the rest of the crowd. They also adore change and excitement and cannot stand boring routine for very long without making a fuss about it.

Of course, if you are in either of the other two groups, you may well not be fully aware of this side of your nature. It is too extrovert for the Settler's liking and not serious and practical enough for the Warrior. But rest assured, *something* of this group is in your subconscious, even if it is only a small part. On the other hand, if the Nomad is your major personality group, you are probably only too well aware that you actually keep some of your wilder urges under strict control!

A few Nomad archetypes are: Wandering Minstrels, Tinkers, Ancient Arabs, Actors, Tricksters, Travellers, Sorcerers, Witches, Warlocks, Wizards, Itinerant Musicians, Soothsayers, False Prophets and Seers, Petty Thieves and Pickpockets, Pirates, Highwaymen, Outlaws, Court Jesters, Storytellers, Dancers, Magicians and Conjurors, Illusionists.

Once again, just allow images to drift through your mind without trying to make it happen. The Nomad is an elusive character, there one moment and gone the next; he or she can be difficult to pin down, even when you are predominantly a Nomad yourself. The Nomad archetype is somewhat different to the modern Nomadic type, in that there is frequently a sense of untrustworthiness, or flashiness that cannot quite live up to its promise. Most modern Nomads have enough Settler or Warrior about them to keep this slightly wild and undisciplined side of their nature properly in check. The great thing about the archetypal Nomad is the sense of fun and spontaneity, and the ability to project their personality well. The modern Nomad who possesses this ability is an individual with real Charisma.

As with the other two groups, use the relaxation routine to help you find your own archetype, the archetype that seems to completely sum up what you understand to be the Nomad. Once you have found your three archetypes, make certain to explore all three individuals, giving them each a personal history if you like. Anything that will make them as real in your imagination as possible will be helpful.

Negative Characters

When you have discovered your three archetypes, you might well find that one of them is a negative character. An example might be the Warrior whose actions are controlled by fear, or who is so dogmatic and inflexible that they refuse to change a plan if a better opportunity presents itself; or the Settler who is timid and unable to stand up for justice, or who agrees with everybody for the sake of a quiet life; or the Nomad who is shifty and unreliable, rather than fun-loving and inspiring.

When this happens, you have discovered a negative aspect of your personality that has been hampering your chances of success, whatever success means to you. The remedy is simple. Do the exercise again for the group(s) where it is necessary, this time searching until you find a *positive* archetype, one who fulfils all that is best about the type. In other words, the Warrior should be brave and direct yet able to adopt strategic change; the Settler communicative and adaptable yet determined to fight for justice; and the Nomad enthusiastic and light-hearted yet at the same time inspiring. Any negative archetype you find will always be around – always has been, in fact – but now you will also have a positive one on which to focus.

Development

Once you have your three positive archetypes, you can use the relaxation routine to continue developing each one, until you know them almost as well as you do your friends and can call them to mind instantly. In this second stage of development, you can take the process further until it feels to you as if this character must have actually existed.

Imagine that you are developing each character for an outstanding TV series and the producer and the actors who play the parts want to know absolutely everything and anything about them: age, height, weight and build; scars or any other distinguishing features; colour of skin, hair and eyes; the clothes they wear. Know the pitch and timbre of their voices, the speed of their movements – whether they are languid and relaxed, or quick and alert, for example – and how they react to other people. How would they react to you?

The Protector

Would the positive Warrior nod approvingly at your usual way of being, or would they sigh in exasperation and try to hurry you up a bit? Is your positive Warrior a schemer able to make faultless plans and bring them to fruition by organising others – or a more hands-on individual who delights in being in the thick of battle, taking on all comers single-handedly if necessary? Or perhaps he or she is somewhere between the two, translating the ideas of others into effective and positive action.

Use your imagination to vividly sense how you would feel if this Warrior was standing in front of you. You should feel that this person would protect you under all circumstances; you should feel safe. If you feel fear or anxiety, then you may be afraid of your own aggressive instincts – after all, this Warrior archetype is a product of your own mind, and those instincts that you are now fearing are therefore present within your psyche. Do not try to do anything about that fear yet, just make a mental note of it.

The Master Communicator

Now, what about the Settler? Is he a patient craftsman or worker of the land, the kind of steady plodder who is totally reliable, if unexciting? Or perhaps she is more dynamic, the lively communicator who excels at teaching the knowledge of life. Maybe his life revolves around art – painting or sculpture for instance. Or perhaps she is a philosopher, making sense of life so that others can enjoy it more.

How would this person react to you? Would she or he like you the way you are, or would they urge you to be more responsible, or perhaps a little more tolerant sometimes? Again, imagine how it would feel if you were physically with this person right this moment. Do you feel comfortably at ease, or do you find something vaguely irritating? If the latter, you might be choosing to disown the gentler and more complicated side of your nature, and perhaps, in addition, seeking to avoid change. You probably *need* change, or you would not be reading this book. Equally, you *need* something of the Settler's way of being if you are going to be truly successful, because to be successful, you need to communicate with others. And, of course, the Settler is the master communicator. Again, there is no need to do anything about that right now, other than to observe it and note it.

Irrepressible Enthusiasm

This brings us to the irrepressibly enthusiastic Nomad. Whatever the type of character, they should be able to create a definite effect within others. Maybe he is an impressive sorcerer, or a joke-a-minute entertainer; a dashing Highwayman, or a vivaciously sparkling Gypsy dancer. Perhaps she can sense the future – or pretend to – or is able to stir the emotions as a consummate actor who can appear to be whatever is required at the time. Whatever, he or she cannot and will not be ignored for more than a few seconds.

And what would the person think of you? Are you fun to be with? Or would there perhaps be a criticism that you were not lively enough, or maybe a touch 'sharp' or overly critical sometimes? And if this individual were to materialise in front of you at this very moment, how would you feel? Delighted with his company? Or would you maybe feel that she needed to 'tone things down' a bit or learn a proper set of values and stop showing off so much? If the latter sums up your thoughts, it may be that you simply do not allow yourself to have fun often enough – or perhaps you just do not allow it to show very easily. You need this aspect of the Nomad's character, because if you are going to be as successful as you can possibly be, you will do it far more easily if you can inspire others to be enthusiastic about your ideas. And when it comes to inspiring others, the Nomad wins hands down.

When you have finished the development of each of your positive archetypes, they will have become so familiar to you that you could describe them to somebody else and make them seem real. The better you know them, how they behave, what they do, how they are, the more help they *are* going to be in your search for success.

Modern Psychology

Modern psychologists know all about these three archetypes – but they may not refer to them by the same names, nor do they all necessarily believe that the behaviour patterns have anything to do with ancestral memories and instincts.

There are numerous different names and styles of personality traits in use today, too many to mention. Listed here are the three that are closest to the Warrior, Settler and Nomad. These terms have been in common use in psychology for very many years but they are so accurate – albeit somewhat negative – that there are very many modern psychologists and psychotherapists who still employ them.

Using these descriptions, the Warrior becomes 'pre-genital, anal group, paranoiac, retentive or obsessional personality'. These terms describe the behaviour and development between the ages of two and five years old, when the urges for control and aggression are revealed. When these urges are predominant in adults, these individuals are often referred to by psychologists by the abbreviated title of 'anal'. In my professional work, I also sometimes use a 'modern' psychological name for the Warrior, referring to it as the 'Resolute Organisational' personality, which I believe is properly descriptive of the way such people are.

Modern psychology labels the Settler 'pre-genital, oral group, schizoid personality'. The name is derived from the behaviour patterns between birth and about two and a half years old; the 'schizoid' part refers to a tendency towards mood swings, and has nothing to do with the catastrophic psychotic illness of schizophrenia. As adults, they will be referred to by psychologists simply as 'oral'. My modern, or professional, name for this group is the Intuitive Adaptable personality – again, it sums up their whole way of being.

The Nomad is known in modern psychology as 'genital group, hysteric personality'. The development phase that this refers to is the early school-age years, and the abbreviated title is 'hysteric'. My modern name is 'Charismatic Evidential', which again describes the 'what you see is what you get' nature of these individuals.

Interaction

By now, you have probably begun to realise that there may well be sides to your personality that you never knew existed. There is a relevant phrase that athletes use to enhance their performance: *If you can see it you can be it.* You should be able to see your three archetypes quite well by now, and since they are the product of your own mind, that athlete's rule applies very well here. Soon you will learn how to easily access the resources associated with each.

But first we have to discover and resolve the subconscious emotional and mental conflicts that almost certainly exist between your three archetypes, because those conflicts are destructive to any form of success.

The next chapter will concentrate on exactly that, and the resolution of those conflicts will give a real 'kick-start' to your quest to find your true self.

Chapter Four
Discovering Conflicts

The personality test in Chapter 2 tells you more than what personality group you are in – your answers also reveal the presence of conflicting urges in the psyche.

These conflicts, where they exist, are evidence of the impossible task that confronts your subconscious every day of your life; the task of attempting to achieve opposite objectives at one and the same time. On a conscious level it would be like trying to reconcile a wish to walk unnoticed through a crowd with an urge to stand under a flashing neon sign announcing "I am here"... or the need to wear lead-weighted diver's boots while attempting to jump over a six-foot-high fence.

Put simply, these conflicts are the result of what you can think of as disagreements between the Warrior, the Settler and the Nomad in your subconscious. This might seem a strange idea, since these archetypes are just creations of your own imagination, but it is an idea that allows you to see clearly how almost invisibly conflict can arise and be disruptive.

Imagine that you are in a confrontational situation with a determinedly aggressive individual. The Settler will be looking for areas of agreement in order to negotiate; the Nomad will be trying to find an escape route; and the Warrior will be seeking a weak area at which to strike. Your course of action may depend upon which is the most dominant aspect of your personality, but the more conflict there is with the other two, the more difficult that task will become. The Settler will be trying to hold the Warrior back, or at least take a calmer approach; the Warrior will be urging the Settler to respond with an aggressively 'hands-on' attitude; and both will be trying to prevent the Nomad from walking away from the situation.

That is an accurate representation of the conflict that can all too easily exist between differing aspects of your personality. Some of those conflicts will be 'built in', i.e. you were born with them, while others will be the result of conditioning or teaching by parents or others during your formative years. These last are nothing more than habits of behaviour, along with perceptions of self and personal worth, that have been imprinted upon your true personality.

This does not mean that your parents or others have set out to give you a poor set of values, but only that their way of being – which they believe is the right way to be and have therefore tried to teach you – simply does not suit the *real* you. So there have probably been many times when you have tried to deal with life in a way that simply does not work for you. We are back to jumping that six-foot fence wearing diver's boots again.

All these conflicts, the built-in ones and those that have been acquired, can be resolved. Most of the time, it is only necessary to identify them and the reason for their existence for this resolution to take place almost automatically, in the depths of the subconscious.

Revelations

So let us begin. The personality test is likely to have revealed your *true* underlying nature, even though that may not agree with the way you have always seen yourself. It may be that when you are introduced to some of the conflicts revealed by your answers, you will want to justify them with a 'Yes, but...' or something similar. Well, 'Yes, but' and 'Ah, but' are both very clear signs of resistance to an idea. For instance, maybe it seems that you can be argumentative in some situations but easygoing in others (questions 4 and 8). Well, *maybe* that is the case; but it is far more likely that you are simply suppressing argumentativeness in certain situations – not the same thing as being easygoing at all. Or maybe you are actually quite easygoing, becoming argumentative about certain things because you feel you should make a stand. Again, it's not really the same thing. A truly argumentative personality argues for the sake of it, likes arguing, and will argue at every opportunity. It is almost a way of life. Easygoing people usually do not see the need for argument and will congratulate themselves on finding a way to avoid one.

42

Sometimes there has been such heavy imprinting that the real self remains hidden. It is easy to find out.

Look at the answers to questions 1, 5 and 9; the scores here should be in the right order. So if, for example, the complete test shows you to be a Warrior first, a Nomad second and a Settler third, then that same order should be reflected in the first question of each group. If this is the case, you know you are on the right track. If it is not, then there is a little 'uncovering' work to do. At this stage, however, there is no need to do anything more with this piece of information, than simply to bear it in mind.

Perhaps all your scores were very close together. If this is also reflected in the first answer to each group, you are either supremely confident and multitalented – and this is not a cynical joke of some sort – or you are negatively oriented, lacking in confidence, have always had great difficulty in working out how to be, what to do and what is right for you, and so on. It makes sense, if you think about it, because all three groups are exerting an equal influence upon you and you literally aren't sure who or what you are supposed to be. Again, do nothing right now other than recognise the fact and bear it in mind. Later in the book, you will discover exactly what work is needed and how to do it. You will then gradually realise that a 'polarising' influence is at work and you will begin to become far more positive.

This really is the easiest way to discover yourself, isn't it? All you have to do is… nothing at all, for most of the time! Where there is work needed, you will discover exactly what to do and how to do it later in the book.

Revelations

To identify conflicts, we need to look at the scores for pairs of questions from each of the relevant groups. The greatest possible difference between them (found only rarely) is 9, the result of a 1 in one group and a 10 in the other. The smaller the difference, the greater the conflict. Adding the two scores together on any pair of questions should give an answer of 10 or more. Anything less than that may indicate negativity, and we will seek to identify exactly where that negative attitude exists.

The 'revelations' shown here all assume that you have a difference between your scores of less than 4, or a combined total of 9 or less. Where this is not the case, you can safely assume you have no conflict in this area.

Warriors v. Settlers

First, we will compare the answers for the Warrior group with those of the Settler. Conflicts here often tend to give rise to any or all of the following: anxiety, panic attacks, feelings of inferiority, phobia, excessive regard for authority figures, depression, indecision, mood swings, mild paranoia.

➤ Questions 1 and 5

1.   *How determined/dogmatic are you?*

5.   *How adaptable/indecisive can you be?*

You cannot be both! If the total is higher than 10, then it is evidence of a conflict between the Warrior's tenacity and determination, and the Settler's ability to find a way around, rather than through, a problem. The higher score tells you which is the more dominant part of your personality, the part you should concentrate on. If they are equal, then you can decide which you feel better about. And you *must* decide, for you will otherwise simply continue the conflict.

If the total is 9 or less, then you lean towards negativity. Once again, the higher number indicates the personality that is most likely to be dominant. This is the positive aspect of that personality, which you should seek, later on.

Now make a note of the positive attribute that has been revealed via this conflict – **determination** or **adaptability**.

➤ *Questions 2 and 6*

2.   *How easily can you 'speak your mind'?*

6.   *How important is it for you to be liked?*

Can you see how mutually exclusive these are? If it truly *is* important for you to be liked, then it is difficult to speak your mind for fear of antagonising someone. Similarly, if you really *can* speak your mind easily, then it cannot possibly matter too much to you what others think of you. This is all about self-belief; your behaviour and confidence will be affected by your belief system, and the more accurate your beliefs about self, the more comfortable you will be.

Where your scores are too close, there are two possibilities:

(1)   Although you are able to speak your mind when necessary, you have to steel yourself to do it, or at least remind yourself that you can and should. Therefore, it is not actually easy at all. Warriors speak their minds without even thinking about it and will sometimes alienate themselves from others. They won't care about that, though!

(2)   Although you want people to like you, you are actually not too concerned when someone does not, and can simply dismiss their opinion as being of no particular importance. If you *truly* need people to like you, then not being *dis*liked would be even more important. Settlers *need* to be liked, since their origins are concerned with harmony and shared effort.

For changes to take place in your subconscious, you will probably need to do nothing more than understand which of the above actually applies to you.

➤ *Questions 3 and 7*

3.   *How shrewd/cynical are you?*

7.   *How reliable/over-trusting can you be?*

These are, of course, complete opposites, so your answers should be widely separated. If they are not, you are probably attempting to adopt an attitude that you have been taught is in some way better than the other. Truly shrewd people will only be reliable when it suits them – in other words, they are not truly reliable. And when things do not pan out the way they should, cynicism is the result, with their shrewdness telling them that they should not have relied on things turning out the way they thought.

Equally, truly reliable people will always do what they have promised or agreed to do, even when it is not in their own best interests – which is far from shrewd! Also, the more reliable they are, the more vulnerable they are to the shrewdness of others. The problem is, if and when they do behave less reliably as a result of temporary shrewdness, their own guilt feelings can give them problems. It is worth realising that as much success has been built upon dependability as upon shrewd far-sightedness.

If the combined total is 10 or higher, then the conflict here is between the Warrior's desire to be in control and the Settler's urge to be dependable. If the combined total is 9 or less, there is likely to be a leaning towards negativity; the higher number and/or the higher score on questions 1 and 5 will tell you which is the most likely positive attribute you should aim for, later on.

Make a note of the dominant urge that you have discovered – **shrewdness** or **reliability**.

➤ *Questions 4 and 8*

4.   *How argumentative can you be?*

8.   *How easygoing are you?*

As a rule, argumentative people are not easygoing! This conflict has been partially discussed earlier in this chapter; the higher answer of the two is likely to indicate the *real* you, particularly if this is confirmed by your scores on questions 1 and 5. Argumentative people demand things their own way most of the time; easygoing people are quite happy to go along with others and suffer less stress in their lives.

A combined total of 9 or less makes little sense here; the less easygoing you are, the more argumentative you will have to be. If you scored as low as this, you are probably hiding from yourself – you may very well be afraid of your own Warrior status! This would give you great difficulty in all areas concerning problem-solving and decision-making, since you will be lacking one coping strategy and not using the other.

It is usually only necessary to understand which attribute truly applies to you for changes to happen.

Settlers v. Nomads

Now we are going to look at the conflict between the Settler and Nomad aspects of your personality. Conflicts here can often give rise to any or all of the following: insecurity, feelings of being a fraud, guilt, petulant or childlike behaviour, shyness/blushing, poor self-image, fear of responsibility, excessive self-consciousness.

➤ *Questions 5 and 9*

5.   *How adaptable/indecisive can you be?*

9.   *How inspiring/over-dramatic can you be?*

You cannot be indecisive and inspiring, nor can you be adaptable and over-dramatic – they are all mutually exclusive. Where there is an apparent conflict here, it is usually because you actually *are* inspiring and over-dramatic but have perhaps been taught that 'inspiring' is flashy or cheap and that 'over-dramatic' is definitely undesirable, maybe even childish. If this is the case, remember that nobody would ever do anything worthwhile if they were not *inspired* to do so by somebody else; and 'over-dramatic' is usually nothing more than the judgement passed upon expressive individuals by those who are less able to show their feelings.

Adaptability, whilst it confers versatility and multiple skills, often carries with it the inability to decide whether to put up with things the way they are or to attempt to make some sort of change. Procrastination sets in, and if this is you, then you will need to work at that later on. Generally, the truly adaptable personality will have scored very low on the other two facets of personality.

A combined total of less than 9 here merely shows some lack of development of character; you will be able to do something about this later.

The higher score on questions 5 and 9 will give you a good indication of the attribute that best applies to you: **inspiring** or **adaptable**.

➤ *Questions 6 and 10*

6.   *How important is it for you to be liked?*

10.   *How easily can you shrug off or ignore criticism?*

These two really do not fit together very well at all; if it is truly important for you to be liked, then any criticism will really sting! You may believe that criticism should not be taken to heart and therefore always make an effort to ignore it, or perhaps you have learned how to counter criticism with comments like "They're only jealous". In either case, you are thinking about it – it matters. If you scarcely notice criticism until somebody else points it out to you, then the opinions of others are less important than you have always believed them to be.

Those who need to be liked usually have a deep understanding of the wishes and needs of others, while the individual who is unperturbed by criticism can achieve much through self-belief.

A low score here indicates that one of your answers may have been less than totally honest! If this is the case, it would be a good idea to sort that out right now – and do not forget to check whether the new answer alters your overall assessment.

The higher score on questions 5 and 9, since they are the 'base' questions for the Settler and Nomad respectively, will give further confirmation or guidance as to your true self; again, it is only necessary to observe this and accept the validity of it for beneficial changes to happen in the subconscious.

➤ *Questions 7 and 11*

7.   *How reliable/over-trusting can you be?*

11.   *How spontaneous/impulsive can you be?*

Whilst there is not so much of a contradiction here as there is with some other conflict situations, it is fair to say that there should be a reasonable separation between the scores and a total of at least 10. Reliable people are not generally very spontaneous – which is, of course, what makes them reliable in the first place, because they tend to think things through before taking action. Spontaneous types, whilst being less reliable, will often make 'snap' decisions with astonishing ease and actually enjoy the risks involved.

A score of 9 or less is likely to indicate the presence of a powerful imprint from parents or others, towards the direction which is *un*suitable, i.e. the urge to be reliable being offset by frequent comments to 'lighten up' or spontaneous actions being met with admonishments along the lines of "You really must learn to look before you leap."

The higher score on questions 5 and 9 (the 'base' questions for the Settler and the Nomad) will indicate your direction if you are uncertain. As a matter of interest, if you *are* uncertain, it is likely that you are more inclined towards reliability.

Make a note of the more likely attribute – **reliability** or **spontaneity**.

➤ *Questions 8 and 12*

8.   *How easygoing are you?*

12.   *How impatient can you be?*

Easygoing individuals are generally unlikely to be impulsively impatient, since very little in life over-excites their calm nature. A conflict here is usually the result of an impulsively impatient individual who *tries* to be easygoing and would actually like to be easygoing and as a result believes that she or he actually *is* easy going! But, when the chips are down, such people want things yesterday – or sooner – and cannot abide the idea of 'marking time' and waiting calmly for things to happen. They are action people who have to get things moving, at which they are often astoundingly successful.

Individuals who are truly easygoing simply take everything in their stride and easily handle any obstacles to their plans. If a task or project is held up due to circumstances beyond their control, they will do what they can, then wait comfortably until work can continue.

Warriors v. Nomads

We are only going to look at the conflict shown by the answers to two questions, here. They are the important ones, and though there can be others (conflicting urges to run and fight, for example) most of them will also be indicated by these two sets of answers.

➤ *Questions 1 and 11*

1.   **How determined/dogmatic can you be?**

11.   **How spontaneous/impulsive can you be?**

This really needs no explanation at all, because if the scores are pretty much equal and the total is 10 or more, then there will be a continuous pull in opposite directions in most areas of life. The

most likely result is the inability to follow up on plans or promises (or threats!), though it may show up as the tendency to come
up with great-sounding schemes that are actually quite viable,
only to have them fail because of a lack of attention to detail. There
may well be relationship difficulties, for a whole host of reasons.
Generally, where there is conflict here, the most likely *genuine*
attribute is **determination**.

A combined total of less than 10 is possible where there is a strong
Settler orientation, in which case it is unimportant, otherwise it is
likely to show a tendency to procrastination and a general weakness of character.

➤ *Questions 3 and 12*

3.   *How shrewd/cynical are you?*

12.   *How impatient can you be?*

A combined total of 9 or less here is not particularly important,
since there are many people who 'fit' somewhere between these
extremes. But their very extremism indicates a big problem if conflict is revealed by close answers and a total of 10 or more.

The effect here is likely to show as hesitation in following instincts,
leading to some very poor decision-making, even though it may
have taken a whole lot of soul-searching to reach those decisions.
There will often be a lot of dissatisfaction with one's self and one's
abilities, coupled with a feeling that others will always be critical,
no matter what.

When spontaneity has ruled, failure will produce self-castigation
along the lines of "I should have known a whole lot better..." Yet
when thought is given and things still don't work out, it'll be something like "I should've just got on with it," or "I don't know why I
thought I could do that". Even when the person is successful, there
will still be self-criticism: "I don't know what on Earth I was thinking of! Thank goodness I got away with it!" or "Yes, but I was so
slow!" There will seldom be real enjoyment of any sort of success,
since self-doubt will almost always be present in the psyche.

Reflections

By now you will probably have discovered areas in your personality that have been in conflict for a good many years. Much of the
time, it is only necessary for those conflict areas to be brought to
conscious awareness for changes to take place in the way you feel,
behave and react, though sometimes it will be necessary to do a bit
of 'homework' to aid the process. An efficient method for carrying
out that particular bit of self-help can be found later on in the
book; for now just content yourself with having discovered more
about yourself than you knew originally. You also have a list (or
should have!) of certain attributes to be developed, attributes that
are part of the *real* you.

As for how awareness of these attributes might change your life
and the way you handle it, read on...

Chapter Five
Archetypes at Work

From this moment onwards, you will be handling life and its problems more easily than ever before. This is because you already have a greater knowledge of who you are, how you work, and why things have not always worked the way you had planned or wished. You have understanding.

Shortly, we are going to have a look at the different ways that your three archetypes would handle certain situations. We will also consider which particular types of circumstances might suit each archetype, how we might sometimes get two, or even all three, to work as a psychological team – and how we might sometimes get one to sit quietly and not interfere!

First, though, we are going to have a look at something else – our belief system and the way it affects our whole life.

Belief and Expectation

What we expect from life, what we believe we will find in life, is governed by the sum total of our experiences in life. It follows, therefore, that the more experience we have – in other words, the longer we have lived – the more of the same we expect to find. That is what makes change so difficult; it can be very difficult indeed to imagine being any way other than how you are. But the belief and expectation system is almost always inaccurate, because it has developed as a result of our behaving (or attempting to behave) *in the way we were taught to,* rather than *in the way that is right for us.*

What do you see written in the triangle above?

If you saw: **'PARIS IN THE SPRING'** – and most people do – then look again. You may have to read it aloud, line by line, before you can see what it actually *does* say…

If you are still certain that it says: **'PARIS IN THE SPRING'**, then your belief system has definitely been 'holding you back'!

What the phrase inside the triangle actually says is:

PARIS IN THE <u>THE</u> SPRING

The reason you didn't see it before is that you did not actually *read* it – you only *looked at* it. 'Paris in the spring' is a well-known phrase, and your belief system insisted that you did not *need* to read it because you already knew what it said just as soon as you saw it.

There are three possibilities:

1. When you looked at the triangle again, you still saw the same thing. You had to have yet another look to confirm the truth.

2. You saw it correctly the second time you looked at it.

3. You saw it correctly straight away.

If the first response applies to you, then you are probably a Nomad, number 2 indicates that you are most likely a Settler, whilst 3 is the strongest indication of the Warrior – unless you had already seen it somewhere before, in which case, try to remember your response the first time around.

The Warrior's response reveals the natural super-observant nature of this personality group; when conflicts have been resolved, this perceptiveness will probably play a large part in eventual success.

Now count the number of times the letter 'F' appears in this short paragraph:

> FINISHED FILES ARE FREQUENTLY
> THE RESULT OF YEARS OF
> SCIENTIFIC RESEARCH.

There are actually six, though most people will see only four, and this time it makes no difference which personality group you are. The chances are that you simply did not count the 'F' in the word 'of', which appears twice – because it *sounds* like a 'V'.

The point of all this is to inject into your belief system something that is very important at this stage, if you are to get the best from this book. That something is a specific form of *DOUBT*. You need a feeling, a growing awareness, that what you have always believed about yourself is worth some reappraisal, so that you can truly open your mind and let go of the barriers that have prevented you, so far, from finding the success you deserve. You need to *DOUBT* that any negative fundamental beliefs you have about yourself have any basis in fact at all. They are no more accurate than what you first believed was written in that triangle or the number of 'F's you counted.

Thinking and Behaviour

There are many times in life when the plans we make are doomed to failure because of an incongruence in our thought and behaviour processes. It is no good *thinking* like a Warrior if you're going to *behave* like a Settler or a Nomad; neither is there much point if you decide to resolve some difficulty or other by talking it through in a calm and rational manner, then get hot around the collar (the Warrior reaction to opposition) if things do not immediately start going the way you wanted them to.

Almost everybody has had the experience whereby private anger has led to a resolution to 'sort out' the person concerned, only to find that when it comes to the event, they simply have not got the resources to sort out anything at all and end up feeling worse as a result! What happens here is simple. You have instinctively recognised, via your ancestral memory traces, that a Warrior approach is called for – and, indeed, it is your Warrior archetype that is being automatically accessed... BUT when you are face to face with the problem, something uncomfortable happens:

You revert to a behaviour pattern that you subconsciously believe is the way you are 'supposed' to be.

Thus the Settler becomes obliging, sometimes fuming inwardly, whilst claiming afterwards that there really was not anything else they could have done, or perhaps insisting that a decent compromise had been agreed. The Nomadic response is either to duck the issue altogether, or to pretend they were not really angry in the first place, then afterwards airily dismissing their ineffectiveness by stating that they have made their point and that was all they wanted to do.

True Warriors, of course, may well survive the encounter with exactly the result that they wanted, but they will find a different problem another time, another place – perhaps going 'OTT' when a 'softly, softly' approach would have achieved a better result.

When you decide on a course of action for any situation, it is important that you either (a) bear in mind your major personality group and plan accordingly, or (b) access the best archetype to give you the resources you need – *and be sure to carry out that course of action in the same mode.* In this way, once you are actually confronted with the situation, your behaviour, thoughts, responses and actions will all be congruent with your preliminary preparations. Or, to put it another way – everything will go according to plan.

A Life Approach

Your whole life can benefit from this approach. Study the way you think about things and the way you would *like* to behave, then compare it with what you actually *do*. The chances are that there is a fair degree of mismatch, so that for much of the time you are frustratedly behaving in a way that is different to how you thought you would behave, how you wanted to behave. No wonder things do not always work out the way you want them to! No wonder you are not able to be as successful as you should be!

And even if you were, how on earth would you recognise success? It would simply not match what you were looking for, since success is always dependent upon the actual *behaviour* that created it, rather than the thoughts that went before it. Any plan we make is mentally tested – or, to put it another way, practised – in our thoughts for the outcome, and if all seems satisfactory, then we proceed. Behave in a different mode to that 'mental test' and it's a bit like setting out on a journey that we planned to make by train but are now making by car… with no map.

You may have conducted almost all of your life so far in that inefficient manner, thinking in the mode that is your natural self but behaving in the mode that you have been taught. There are many give-away signs. The Nomad who behaves as either Settler or Warrior wants to be charismatic and spontaneous but feels unable to be so, exhibiting either disdain or boredom towards those behaviour patterns. The Warrior acting as Nomad or Settler would love to be a leader, or somehow of more consequence, but instead pretends to believe that life is too short to bother with such things, or that he or she is 'having plenty of fun with things just the way they are, thank you'. Settlers whose instincts have been suppressed by Warrior or Nomad behaviour will wish they had a bigger circle of friends or greater popularity but keep those feelings, and all others, a close secret.

In a nutshell, you can think about being successful as much and as often as you like. But only *doing* stuff in the way that you think about it will produce that success.

Natural Resources

The resources of your major personality group are the easiest for you to access – even if you have behaved in a different mode up until now. Always try to achieve your aims and goals or solve any of life's difficulties in that mode, since that is the way you are designed to operate, and the way you are most likely to find success, whatever task you are tackling. Many times, you will find that you need to do nothing more than *truly* be yourself, though you may need a bit of practice at first.

If you think like a Warrior, then be sure your behaviour is aimed at maintaining control of self and situations without resorting to aggression; use determination, manipulation, speed of thought, exploitation of weaknesses in any adversary's argument or stance. Aggression simply creates a confrontational situation where there are usually no winners.

If you think like a Settler, then use your skills of communication and understanding to enhance your natural friendliness; people generally respond well to people who like them and to people who *are* like them, so you might also bring your versatility and adaptability into play. Stand firm against any suggestion that you should ever settle for a lesser result than you know to be fair.

If you think in Nomad mode, the best way for you to handle anything is to make it clean, quick and easy. Use light-heartedness where it is appropriate; exude confidence, even if you have to put on an act, and be sure to use your inspirational powers to the full. You can easily make people smile, and there are few situations where this is not an asset.

Of course, there will always be occasions when your natural mode simply is not the best one for the task at hand, and that is where the ability to 'switch on' what you need is very powerful indeed.

The Vivid Mental Image

We are going to examine the usefulness of applying the resources of each archetype to everyday events and situations, and how you can use the knowledge you already have to improve your own reactions. The way to get the best out of any situation is to work out where you will find the greatest advantage. Think about these abbreviated character descriptions: the Warrior is **Forceful, Resolute, Organisational**; the Settler is a **Sociable, Intuitive** and **Adaptable** character; while the Nomad is **Restless, Charismatic** and **Innovative**.

Within those traits are the reactions and behaviour set you need for just about every situation you will find in life. Accessing them is easy enough – you already have a very clear image of and 'feel' for each archetype; now all you need to do is to create a truly Vivid Mental Image – or VMI for short – of that individual, *and recognise how his or her resources are applicable to the situation in hand.* Notice that you are simply going to use the resources of your archetype, not attempt to actually *be* like him or her. An ancient Warrior, for instance, would not fit in too well at a company board meeting – but an individual with the methodical thought processes, perception and resolve of the Warrior archetype most definitely would. The resources of your archetypes are every bit as valid in the modern world as they were in the ancient one.

When you create your VMI and hold it for a few seconds (the length of time needed for maximum effect decreases with practice) *with the intention of using the associated mode of behaviour,* you automatically activate the resources you need, deep in your subconscious mind. Then you can simply forget it. There really is nothing else you need to do – it's that easy. What actually happens is that your subconscious will make minor changes in your body language, your speech, breathing rate and other almost invisible signals. Others will react appropriately, responding at a subconscious level to whatever signals you 'send', be it the firm resolve of the Warrior, the friendly sociability of the Settler, or the enthusiasm of the Nomad. Even when your basic personality is the best one for the situation, it can be a worthwhile exercise to create the VMI, since this will strengthen your positive traits.

Remember, it is behaviour patterns that will change, not your actual thought processes. You will always remain yourself within yourself, because we are not attempting some Jekyll/Hyde conversion!

How does it Feel?

When the VMI is generated, there is usually a momentary awareness of change or difference, which normally lasts for a few
seconds at most. This is your subconscious acceptance of the
behaviour mode. But because the processes of our subconscious
are completely 'invisible' to our conscious mind, we may not be
aware that the resources we have accessed are actually available to
us until they are needed. Just the fact that they are there may be all
that is necessary for us to achieve our objectives, so it is important
to recognise that if you do not feel very different (though many do)
it does not mean that the process isn't working. It is also possible
that whatever changes you do experience will appear so natural
that they might not seem to be anything more than a different
aspect of your normal self. After all, you are only accessing attributes that are already part of the real you, even though they might
have been woefully underused until now. You will not necessarily
seem noticeably different to others at first, either (though, again,
many do) because the adjustment to your behaviour patterns may
be very subtle.

It is when the particular resource is needed that the surprise happens – because it is suddenly just there, in your mind and in your
body, and it is then that you become aware that something is *truly*
different. It tends to have a distinct feeling of "Well! I couldn't
have done *that* before…"

The beauty of all this, of course, is that you do not have to remember anything or sustain anything; your subconscious mind will
ensure that your behaviour is in tune with your deepest thought
processes so that it becomes a natural way for you to be. The most
noticeable difference from the outside is that you will seem more
confident and at ease with yourself. But the most noticeable
change from the inside will be that things begin to go just the way
you want them to, just the way you have planned.

In the branch of modern psychology known as NLP (Neuro-
Linguistic Programming), the VMI would be known as an 'anchor'
to positive resources, and it is recognised as a very powerful
method of achieving excellence. The only exception to all this is
the rare situation where one of your archetypes showed as less

than 20 per cent of your personality. In these cases, it is better to rely on the strengths of the other two; it is a good idea, anyway, to use your two highest groups as much of the time as you can.

Horses for Courses

Now we will have a detailed look at a common situation which, though it is really only a petty irritation, can sometimes be literally deadly. Imagine that you are driving in a slow-moving line of traffic when somebody jumps the queue by travelling down the wrong lane and then pulling sharply in front of you. There are three different courses of action that are most likely to be taken in these circumstances:

1. Sound your horn and gesticulate wildly and insultingly. If it is dark, put your headlamps on full beam to punish the offending driver.

2. Attempt to close the gap in front of you to stop the other driver from getting in, then fume and resolve to get even when you do not manage it. 'Tailgate' the offending driver as long as you are behind him or her.

3. Feel irritated, but drop back to make room for the other car.

Now, you might guess that the responses are, in order, Nomad, Warrior and Settler. It is easy to see which is the most sensible reaction, but what would you *actually* do (and be honest)?

Adopting the Right Mode

If the answer is either 1 or 2, then consider this: if that driving behaviour irritates you so much, it might be because you sometimes have a tendency or secret wish to do that very thing yourself; it is most likely to be inspired by the Warrior's aggression or the Nomad's impulsive impatience. Far better to adopt the Settler mode of behaviour, with option number 3. Drop back, make room, and prove what you already know – you are a better driver.

61

Of course, you would have already 'adopted' Settler mode before setting out on your journey, since it is obvious that the calmness and adaptability of that archetype is far more suited to the task in hand than either the aggression of the Warrior or the excitability of the Nomad.

But suppose your predominant personality is *not* Settler – suppose, for example, that you are 40 per cent Warrior and only 25 per cent Settler? Well, that is actually an easy situation. Warriors are quick to see advantages and make use of the attributes of others – so you can simply recognise that you are going to *use* the Settler's abilities to your benefit to demonstrate just how unruffled you can be, how much in control of your situation. If you are a Nomad, then the Settler mode can easily be acquired (acted, if you like), because that allows you to demonstrate that you are one of the best drivers on the road.

At first, it may be necessary for you to remember that you are in Settler mode from time to time and in different road situations; with practice, though, you will automatically adopt it every time you drive, and the act of driving itself will become a trigger for Settler behaviour patterns. Or, to put it more simply, you will learn a new and better habitual driving style. You will automatically be more tolerant, less stressed, less likely to have an accident, and less likely to have a raised insurance premium – to name just a few benefits.

Of course, you have to *want* to adopt that new habit…

It is worth recognising that an individual who is predominantly Warrior, for example, will certainly display Warrior resources in greater depth than a Settler or Nomad who has adopted the mode. But that Settler or Nomad will still fare better with the adopted behaviour, when it is needed, than he or she would have done without it.

Common Situations

Here are some common situations in which there are advantages to be gained by adopting specific modes of behaviour. Answer each question with a W, S or N to indicate what you perceive as being the best *single* archetype to handle the situation. Give as much thought as you like to each; there is no need to rush, and it is a good idea to mentally project each archetype into each situation to see which one copes best. Later, as you practice more and more, you will find yourself quickly realising which to use. Later still, you won't even have to think about it at all – it will become a completely automatic process.

Do the test first, then read on to see how accurate you were.

1.   An interview with your bank manager concerning a loan/mortgage.

2.   Giving a speech at a wedding reception or birthday party.

3.   Helping a friend/relative to deal with relationship problems.

4.   Selling your house, car, or some other major item.

5.   Dealing with a difficult neighbour.

6.   Attending a job interview.

Answers

1. *An interview with the bank manager.*

Warriors will usually do very well here, as long as they don't attempt to use aggression. The resources that need to come into play here are perceptiveness, level-headedness and practicality. The lack of animated body language is quite often read as self-confidence and a cool head, while the tendency to think things through impartially before making a commitment – or indeed, applying in the first place – will often result in the best possible 'deal' being obtained.

The Settler, although an expert at communication and negotiation, may not do as well here; Settlers are more likely to work out how or if they can afford the required repayments, rather than standing firm for a lower interest rate or a longer repayment term. Also, the Settler's need to be liked can lead to anxiety about the manager's personal reactions, whereas this sort of matter is more effectively handled at a purely impersonal and factual level.

Although usually very personable, the Nomad would probably be the least suitable of all, since the Nomad's high enthusiasm can suggest a lack of practicality to some people. Also, the Nomad's somewhat impulsive approach to life means that plans and applications may not be thought through well enough to stand up to close scrutiny.

2. *Giving a speech at a wedding reception or birthday party.*

This is where the Nomad will excel, of course! The generally light-hearted attitude and sense of fun, along with a lack of self-consciousness and a natural ability to play to the audience, means that the Nomad will usually deliver an entertaining and lively discourse, quite often 'off the cuff'. There is frequently a natural flair for acting and telling stories and jokes, as well as a knack for impressing the audience by making the whole thing look easy. Most importantly, the Nomad personality will truly enjoy the experience, and the audience will share that enjoyment.

The Warrior can actually do quite well with this sort of thing, as long as the audience appreciates a dry sense of humour. It is unlikely that there will be much in the way of sparkling wit – instead, expect a more subtle approach, with a few carefully observed amusing remarks about the subject of the party. The biggest problem is likely to be one of brevity – the speech may be short, and not too sweet.

Settlers will often have problems of confidence here, since they do not usually like to be 'in the limelight'. This can result in the speech simply not coming across very well, no matter how well written; the audience may well sense the nervousness and find themselves feeling awkward for the speaker.

3. *Helping a friend or relative to deal with relationship problems.*

In many ways, this is a bit of a trick question, because, to a large extent, the answer depends on the personality of the friend or relative.

Overall, though, this is very much the domain of the Settler. Their natural sensitivity to the feelings of others means Settlers are uniquely equipped to offer a near-perfect balance of understanding and practical help for almost anybody. Their versatility and adaptability means that they are likely to be able to find a solution to most difficulties, or, at least to come up with an action plan to boost and sustain flagging spirits. They will usually also be able to see how the problems have arisen in the first place and offer advice there, too.

Nomads can do well here – but only on a superficial level, lifting the spirits by force of personality alone. This lifting of spirits will usually evaporate when they leave, though, since they do not usually have the insight necessary to find workable answers to the underlying difficulties within a relationship. Their major asset in this situation is the ability to impart a feeling that things are not quite as bad as they seem.

Warriors can also help here, albeit usually somewhat gruffly and with a down-to-earth, no-nonsense approach not based very much on sympathy. Warriors are a little short on sympathy but high on practicality and will be inclined to offer advice about how to deal with the current situation rather than finding ways to improve it.

4. *Selling your house, car, or some other major item.*

This is Nomad territory! The ability to inspire and enthuse others really comes into its own here, and there are none better than the Nomad when it comes to sparking the imagination into a forward projection of the joys and advantages of ownership. There are few who do not warm to them, as when Nomads are in good form, their natural enthusiasm is infectious. They also possess a tremendous ability to extol virtues and assets whilst easily glossing over any negative aspects.

Warriors do not fare nearly so well here, because of their cynicism. They are likely to harbour a feeling that any 'prospects' may be wasting their time, and the resultant coolness (with some Warrior types this would also be emphasised with strangers) will seem unwelcoming. In addition, Warriors are usually not very talkative, and this can make it seem as if they have something to hide.

Settlers should definitely rely on a professional to sell anything! They will be an easy touch for bargaining, especially if confronted with a Warrior type (or somebody who has read this book!), and will all too often easily be persuaded to go beneath their 'lowest offer' threshold. It is even possible that if they take a liking to their 'customers' they will actually *offer* a lower price at the first sign of any hesitation.

5. *Dealing with a difficult neighbour.*

The Warrior in 'polite mode' is the only one who is pretty much certain to be effective in this situation. Firmness and a practical, no-nonsense attitude can never offend anybody, nor will it leave any doubt that whatever behaviour is being complained about – if the complaint is justified – will have to be altered in some way. The Warrior's cool manner and lack of concern about being liked is very effective here, since there is nothing to trade on or take advantage of.

The Settler can sometimes get quite good results, as long as the neighbour has a 'better self' to appeal to, or a sense of justice that can be acted upon. Generally, though, this personality will open such confrontation with "I'm sorry to be a nuisance..." or something similar. After that, you can forget getting your own way. After all, *you've* already done the apologising!

Nomads will always be too expressive to handle this sort of situation particularly well – they are likely to meet aggression with aggression or a hasty back-down, and any apology or agreement on the neighbour's part will often produce an irritating and provocative "I should damn well think so!" type of response. You have already learned that Nomads are inspiring – but nobody has said that they will always inspire the reaction they want. In this case it is very likely to be retaliation.

6. *Attending a job interview.*

This is another 'trick' question, impossible to answer correctly *or* incorrectly, because it depends so much upon the type of job you are applying for.

Generally speaking, the higher the position, the more Warrior characteristics would be suitable; higher positions usually need a degree of independent thought, and independence is a strong feature of most Warrior types. It is worth remembering though, that you would need to show the attributes desirable for the work, so an applicant for a sales position who shows the expansiveness of the Nomad, for example, is going to be more favourably perceived than an individual with the typical Settler's obliging and slightly reserved manner. The personality of the interviewer comes into play to an extent, too. You would need to be direct with a Warrior, enthusiastic with a Nomad and 'chatty' if you were talking to a Settler type.

Easy Reminders

With any situation that requires you to use an 'adopted mode' – and driving is a good example, where the Warrior surfaces within most people so easily and abruptly – it may be necessary, from time to time, to remind yourself of the archetype you have accessed, and why. All that is necessary is to re-create, for just a split second, the VMI of the archetype you need; at that point you will be aware of the change and this will be sufficient to fully re-establish the mode.

Multiple Modes

Sometimes you may see a benefit in using two or even all three archetypes at the same time; this is not difficult to achieve. Selling is a good example – if you have the communication of the Settler, the enthusiasm of the Nomad and the resolve of the Warrior, you can probably sell ice to an Eskimo! In this case, you would simply visualise the Nomad being in charge, with the other two backing him up. Your VMI could be just that, in fact – the Nomad standing in front of the other two, while they look on, ready to intervene if necessary. With practice you will be able to easily switch between them as you feel the need; there is more about this later on.

Finally, just as there are times when it is useful to combine strengths, there are other circumstances where your major archetype may be a hindrance – the Settler having to deal with that difficult neighbour is a good example. In these cases, you would need to create a VMI of the appropriate archetype completely separate from and independent of the other two – you could, for instance, visualise the others as being sound asleep.

At first, you will probably need a degree of thought and inventiveness to get the best results from this process of accessing your ancestral memories and instincts when you need them. After just a bit of practice, however, it will become second nature. After all, they *are* all just aspects of yourself.

In the next chapter, we will look at the negative effects that your earliest influences have had upon your belief system… and learn how to overcome them.

Chapter Six
Never Too Late

In this chapter we are going to look at the way your fundamental belief system about yourself developed, and how you can change it for the better. We will also examine how you can use past errors and inadequacies to actually increase your chances of success in the future.

First, though, it is important to recognise that, while we are going to investigate the effect that the beliefs and teachings of parents or parent figures have had upon your true self, we are not accusing anybody of being responsible for any of your current difficulties. Indeed, even if anybody *was* entirely responsible for your way of being, there would be little point in attributing blame, since this would achieve nothing. Instead we will simply look for the most likely negative effects you have suffered, then set about putting them right.

The term 'parent figures' refers to those people who brought you up and looked after you (or not!) and can include grandparents, foster parents, adoptive parents, step-parents, guardians, etc. If you grew up in an orphanage or other institutionalised environment, then just think of the individual who seems to you to have had the most impact upon you during your time there.

Of course, you will have been subject to the ministrations of many other people in your early years, but their influences will have had less depth and therefore be of less effect on your general way of being. In a later chapter, we will investigate their possible influences, but it is worth recognising that if a teacher, for example, seems to have had a very profound effect upon your life (whether that effect was good or bad), it is most likely because she or he exhibited a behaviour pattern with which you were already familiar. People sometimes dispute this, but further investigation almost always shows it to be true. It is sometimes easier to admit that a teacher does not seem to like you very much than it is to accept the same of a parent.

Make No Allowances

To get the best from this exercise, it is important that you make no allowances for anybody or justify their behaviour in any way; nor should you allow your initial thoughts to be tempered by the fact that you now recognise that things were not always as they seemed, or that there were circumstances which you were not able to fully appreciate. What is *absolutely essential* is that you recapture the way things actually seemed to you at the time, because how they *seemed* to you is how they *were* as far as your developing mind was concerned. The fact that everything may look less uncomfortable in retrospect is simply an indication that the conflict that existed has had its negative effect upon you – or to put it another way, you have given in.

Remember, we are not blaming anybody for anything; we are simply establishing the mode in which you were taught to think and behave, then using that information to produce a beneficial change for your life *now*. If you still feel uneasy about admitting negative parental influences because of feelings of loyalty, or because you are certain that they had only your best interests at heart, then consider this: if they deserve such loyalty or if they did only have your best interests at heart, wouldn't they now want you to do whatever is necessary to have the best life you can? If you have difficulty answering that question, then you may be hiding from an uncomfortable truth.

A Clear Picture

To begin our task, we have to get a clear picture of the influences that were applied. This is actually a lot easier than it seems, because all we need to know is whether the predominance was towards Warrior, Settler or Nomad. The answers to a few simple questions will tell us just that. First, decide which parent made most impression on your life in those early years, and answer the questions based on that parent's attitudes. If you feel that they were both equally influential, then answer the questions for both.

In the five questions that follow, you will find three groups of character attributes listed; we are going to use your answers to discover the major influences that were applied during your formative years. Study the attributes, then answer each question as spontaneously as you can with a W, S or N. Bear in mind that only one or two of the listed traits in any one group may have been evident, and choose the group that is *most like* that parent. If you grew up in a 'depersonalised' environment like a children's home, then you can simply choose the attitudes that seemed to be most prevalent.

Question 1. *In general, which of the following best describes your more influential parent?*

Warrior: Strong, strict, unyielding, aloof, unemotional, distant morose.
Settler: Kind, forgiving, affectionate, happy, shy, melancholy, defeatist.
Nomad: Fun, boisterous, flashy, loud, a show-off, appearance-oriented.

Question 2. *If you were upset or distressed for some reason, which of the following would be your influential parent's most likely reaction?*

Warrior: Dismissive, disinterested, irritated/angry, unsupportive.
Settler: Comforting, helpful, reassuring, 'making it better', soothing.
Nomad: Jokes, avoiding the issue, diverting attention, "When I was your age...".

Question 3. *When you were in conflict with your parent(s), which of the following would have been the most likely response?*

Warrior: Hitting/slapping etc., domination, withdrawal of privileges, bribes.
Settler: Pleading, coaxing, not talking, martyrdom, appealing to better self.
Nomad: Threats to leave, embarrass you, feign illness, 'pass the buck'.

Question 4. *If a large problem or difficulty that in some way involved you suddenly became apparent, how would your parent(s) react?*

Warrior: Logical, practical, efficient, dogmatic, down-to-earth.
Settler: Emotional, intuitive, optimistic, unassertive, weak.
Nomad: Exaggerate/dramatise, bluster, deny responsibility, self-interest.

Question 5. *On special occasions – day-trips and outings, school sports and plays, birthdays and the like – what would be the most likely attitude?*

Warrior: Bored, complaining, non-participatory, silent, inexpressive.
Settler: Encouraging, supportive, participatory, anxious, doubtful.
Nomad: Enthusiastic, excited, inspirational, claiming credit.

Taking Stock

You should now be able to clearly see the major influences on your formative years, simply by counting up the number of W, S and N responses you have written down. There are, however three possibilities worth considering, which may or not apply to your own assessment.

1. *There is a notable absence of one of the influences.*

When this is your own major personality group, there were probably many misunderstandings and communication difficulties between you and your parents and you will find truly *enormous* benefits from working with this book. If, however, the missing group is the smallest part of your personality, then the associated archetype may well need a bit of extra development before you can use it effectively.

2. *There is no obviously dominant influence (2 W, 4 S, 4 N, for example).*

In this case, give dominance to the order of W, N, S, so that in the example above, you would assume the major influence to be Nomadic. The reason for this order of dominance is that Warrior and Nomad basic drives are both more concerned with the

fundamentals of existence than those of the Settler; the most powerful urge that we have is towards *survival* (the Warrior's basic
motivator), followed by *pleasure* (very much the domain of the
Nomad, of course) and finally, *security*, beloved of the gentle
Settler.

3. *You had difficulty in answering the questions because the responses of
one or both parents were totally inconsistent.*

Here, a great deal of careful, thorough work needs to be done;
your parents' apparent inconsistency is likely to have left you with
a great deal of uncertainty about how you should be, what sort of
aims you should pursue, and how you should go about achieving
them. The advantage here is that your own natural resources will
have been left unfocused but pretty much intact, and you will start
to be feel them more powerfully once uncertainty begins to diminish – which has quite probably already started happening.

Imprints and Instincts

Now we are going to assess the most likely problems that have
been created by parental imprints upon your basic personality, by
studying the relevant parent/child combination in the list that follows. For instance, if your major personality is Warrior and your
parental influences appear to have been largely Nomad, then you
would look under the heading "Warrior Personality – Nomad
Parent" to understand both the likely effects and what you need to
do to overcome them. You should make a note of the passages in
italics that apply to you; later on we will be basing your self-
therapy plan on these comments.

➤ *Warrior Personality*/Nomad Parent

The Warrior personality is based on fear and aggression, and
Nomadic behaviour patterns imprinted onto Warrior instincts
may create an individual who will have few inhibitions in using
their naturally aggressive tendencies to safeguard their interests
and get their own way. They will often trade on the fear of others,
and there can be a basic selfishness that may lead to behaviour that

can seem totally outrageous. Generally speaking, this individual is likely to have the tenacity and determination to actually do all the dramatic things he or she has heard the parent say they would do, or would like to do.

Work should be on control issues, introducing the ideas of (1) delaying gratification for greater end reward; and (2) restraint when dealing with others, to maintain more complete control of awkward situations.

➤ *Warrior Personality*/Settler Parent

Settler traits of tolerance, adaptability and responsiveness to the needs of others being imprinted onto the Warrior personality can lead to severe subconscious conflict between the urge to control and the urge to please, often leading to excessive self-control. Subsequent attempts to suppress aggressive or dominant behaviour may result in guilt feelings; in this case there will be a need to find a benign way to discharge physical urges normally associated with aggression, which may result in obsessive behaviour patterns. The fundamental belief that the Warrior's major facility – channelled aggression – should be kept in check can result in feelings of inadequacy or an inability to cope. Numerous failed attempts to adapt to situations and the needs of others, along with tolerance enforced by the parent, create high levels of frustration; this, in turn, may be responsible for a quick temper and covert manipulation of situations, which can sometimes show as slyness or deceitfulness.

Work on controlled assertiveness and the idea that people generally respond well to those who can take decisions easily and keep control of situations. Learn to use inner resources for greater control generally.

➤ *Warrior Personality*/Warrior Parent

This is the circumstance where having the same major influence and birth predisposition is not necessarily conducive to healthy emotional development. If the parent is a confident individual, then there should be no underlying problems, and the child will usually grow up to be confident and positive. He or she will be straightforward and direct, though often with double standards –

one rule for self and a different one for others. But if the parent has a need to exert continual control, then the child may develop the typical Warrior selfishness, sly or crafty behaviour patterns, and/or a profoundly dogmatic, stubborn and dictatorial manner. Either way, there will usually be a deep and unshakeable inner belief (often correct) that she or he is quicker-thinking than many others.

Work needs to be centred around the idea that whilst tenacity is a positive and useful attribute, obstinacy or stubbornness invariably leads to failure. There is a need to recognise the value of flexibility in dealing with others.

➤ *Settler Personality*/Warrior Parent

The Settler personality is based on love and security, and interaction with others. The imprint of the parental tendencies to tackle adversity with a directly confrontational approach are in severe conflict with the Settler ancestral instincts for tolerance, adaptability and reconciliation, and deep feelings of inadequacy may result. Lack of emotional response from the parent can result in feelings of inferiority and lack of self-worth, which are exacerbated by lack of encouragement for endeavours. There will often be an almost totally negative, pre-defeated attitude to life which, coupled with unexpressed anger, may result in melancholia or depression. There will usually be great difficulty with assertiveness and saying 'no' when necessary, and there is also likely to be excessive subservience or regard for authority figures. There is frequently a noticeable lack of initiative.

*Work on self-worth, assertiveness, and positive thought processes, along with the idea that the opinions and actions of others are only a product of **their** own thoughts and are of no particular importance. Encourage the notion that a conscientious approach to life is wasted if it is not used in some way.*

➤ *Settler Personality*/Nomad Parent

Nomadic instincts and behaviour patterns, imprinted onto the home-loving and conscientious attitude of the Settler personality, tend to create the roots of deep insecurity; this is exacerbated as the child begins to perceive that the parent does not always do what he or she has promised, and that there are other areas of unreliability. As the child attempts to emulate the imprinted behaviour set there is subconscious conflict between belief and instinct, the conscious mind often finding the need to loudly justify areas where the individual perceives that he or she has exercised too little thought or consideration. When things go wrong, there will be a tendency to overreact and to exhibit an 'all or nothing' response along with deep concern over what other people may think. There is often excessive concern about even minor social gaffes and an over-apologetic attitude to mistakes of any sort.

Work particularly on confidence, self-worth, and security issues, and promote the idea that mistakes are invaluable aids for learning and self-improvement. Use visualisation techniques to enhance physical self-image, which is almost always inaccurate in some way.

➤ *Settler Personality*/Settler Parent

Usually among the happiest of people, there is frequently a high degree of tolerance towards others along with an easy, unassuming and usually modest manner. Typical problems can include a lack of ambition and/or tenacity, a tendency to be too trusting, and an inability to understand or predict the actions of less pleasant personalities. Though self-confidence is usually quite good, there can be self-doubt in specific areas; usually this is based on experience rather than fear and creates a tendency towards under-achievement.

Work on positive thought issues and the ability to learn from error and experience, with growth and improvement arising from the knowledge gained.

➤ *Nomad Personality*/Warrior Parent

The Nomad personality is based on the pleasure principle – self-gratification, novelty, and excitement or drama. The Warrior imprint can easily make for a bullying individual who is inclined to bluster and threaten in order to get his or her own way but doesn't have the courage or resources to follow up; there may also be a tendency to make many plans, which are boasted about but never actually implemented or brought to completion. The parent's tendency to emotional coolness may encourage the belief that it is necessary to exaggerate everything in order to gain acceptance, encouragement or attention. Eventually, telling the tale well may be more important than doing the deed at all. As a result, this individual may also be likely to claim special skills and powers, peculiar illnesses or bodily conditions, or indulge in the continual telling of outlandish tall tales. There will usually be an urge to deny that any form of personality assessment is even partly accurate.

Work on the benefits of popularity, developing the idea that people like best those who are fun to be with and who can be relied upon to present a cheerful front. Be ultra-aware that popularity and pleasure are easily gained by following through on plans and promises.

> ➤ *Nomad Personality*/Settler Parent

The ancestral memory traces of Nomadic instincts in the child, in conflict with the nurturing, home-loving and conciliatory attitudes of the parent, will tend to create feelings of boredom, a resultant low concentration threshold, and a feeling of being thwarted in their wish for excitement. Parental overreaction to the resultant super-dramatic outburst may teach this individual that tantrums are rewarded by gratification as the parent strives to create happiness and security for the child; in this way, this personality is encouraged to expect that continual complaints, arguments or demands, with no concerns about mundane issues such as discipline, will produce desirable results. This individual may therefore exhibit extremely selfish behaviour patterns and have difficulty conforming to social norms or accepting that they cannot simply have what they want without earning it.

Work on self-sufficiency and the fact that this will impress others, as well as on the idea of becoming your own person, at least the equal of any other. Remember that creativity and inventiveness can easily be used for personal gain. Individuality and independence are enormously strong attributes.

➤ Nomad Personality/Nomad Parent

Here, the parental influences exacerbate the birth predisposition, heightening the Nomad patterns to the extent that the other two groups have little or no modifying effect. The result is a high-energy individual, usually with consummate acting skills, which may occasionally be used to get his or her own way if all else fails. There is frequently a great deal of exuberance, and some difficulty in understanding that not everybody shares the same outrageous or boisterous sense of fun. There is a built-in ability to switch rapidly between concepts, plans and ideas, though this may well irritate others who are involved with them.

Work on enhancing the positive attributes of your second group. In this way, your natural energy levels will help you to achieve much, via the resolve of the Warrior or the conscientiousness of the Settler, that would normally be unavailable to you.

Success where you Want it...

By now, you are beginning to get a far clearer picture of the work you need to do to make great improvements to your life – to achieve success just where you want it. If you want to be successful in business, gain promotion at work or even strike out on your own, that can happen. If you simply want to feel more confident within yourself, then that will happen automatically – it can't *not*, in fact! If you want to improve your relationships, or even start a new one, then you can do that, too. And if your problem is that you are not really sure what you want from life, then that can and will soon start to change.

But we need one more fact in place before we can begin. We need a new look at some past difficulties, inadequacies, even failures during your adult years. It does not matter a great deal in what area of life we find them, but it is important that (a) the negative outcome was at least partly your own fault; and (b) your recall of the situation is fairly clear. Most people will find a memory presenting itself fairly quickly; if you find yourself with several, then choose the one that feels worst to start with.

In the unlikely event that you simply cannot find anything that is at least partly attributable to your own contribution, then ask yourself why you are reading this book – you must already be nearly perfect! If this genuinely seems to be the case, there is something important you should consider. If things only go wrong for you because of what other people do, you are in real trouble, because you cannot change that situation. You *need* to have a faulty behaviour pattern in some way, otherwise you are stuck with what you already have, since it cannot be improved upon. So have another look at some of those situations where you have been 'let down', where you 'carried the can', did not have the right background, were duped, taken in, or whatever other reasons you have used to defend yourself. You are fooling nobody but yourself if you continue to truly believe that you could not have done anything to alter the outcome of the situation. In fact, if that were true, that statement itself would be an admission of your ineffectiveness.

If you have difficulty obtaining a clear impression or memory, then you can use the concentration enhancer, or the self-hypnosis that you will learn in Chapter Eight, to help. Just focus on the memory and without working at it, allow your mind simply to drift in and out of the concepts, situations, people and ideas that present themselves to you.

Once your thoughts are clear and focused, let yourself realise and accept what you did wrong, how you mishandled the situation. You will find negative attitudes that will be specific to the mode in which you were operating at the time. Some examples might be:

Warrior: too aggressive, too obstinate or pedantic, refusing advice, refusing to delegate work or responsibility, too critical, too selfish or greedy, impatient, distrustful, resistant to change, too controlling, too aloof.

Settler: too trusting, inability to say 'no', unassertiveness, giving up too easily, problems with decisions, too easily influenced, lack of self-belief, feelings of failure, errors in planning, control problems, shyness, ineffectiveness.

Nomad: irresponsibility, carelessness, impulsiveness, lack of planning, lack of consideration, low tenacity, thoughtlessness, boasting, being over-dramatic, lying, poor concentration, lack of application, fickleness.

Now that you have the clearest picture you can create of how your own negativity caused your problems, you can consider how the outcome might have been if you had:

(a) Behaved in the same mode but using the positive resources.

(b) Behaved in your *true* personality mode.

(c) Behaved in an archetypal mode that was more suitable.

With just a bit of of thought, you should soon recognise that you could have achieved a better result if you had known then what you know now. This is an honest recognition that you were responsible, at least in part, for your own downfall; it should not be a negative experience, because you now recognise that you have far more control over your life and your destiny. That recognition is not just through the benefit of hindsight, of course, but is also due to the effect of new and exciting knowledge being brought to bear.

Examine the situation thoroughly – with interest and enthusiasm rather than with regret or self-deprecation; this is a learning experience that will help you to be successful in life, whatever success means to you. It is only when you are able to easily and confidently accept responsibility for your own actions that you can learn from error, and understanding clearly what went wrong gives you the best possible chance of getting it right next time.

Repeat the exercise for as many 'failure' memories as you wish; each one is practice at accessing the archetype that would be best suited to events, using real-life situations that are or were directly applicable to your way of being. It can only serve to strengthen your use of your true ancestral memories, and will actually help to increase your personal confidence and self-belief.

So now you have an awareness of how you can easily be more in control of your life, along with a list of attributes to develop (from Chapter Four) and a knowledge of the fundamental work to be carried out on your personal belief system. The concentration enhancer from Chapter Three is an excellent tool to help you in that task, and later in the book you will learn an even more powerful agent for change, in the form of self-hypnosis.

Chapter Seven
The Magical Power
of Visualisation

By now, you will have certain objectives in mind, as well as the information and skills to achieve them. To recap, you can now:

1.   Fully develop the positive aspects associated with your major personality group, Warrior, Settler or Nomad.

2.   Finally resolve the conflicts that were revealed in Chapter Four, allowing you to increase your natural abilities to be reliable, spontaneous, inspiring, adaptable, shrewd or determined.

3.   'Recondition' your fundamental belief system, as outlined in Chapter Six.

Visualisation

All three of those objectives are going to be attained with the help of either the concentration enhancer from Chapter Three, or the self-hypnosis method set out in Chapter Eight. You will also be using a skill that you already have – visualisation. You have already had a fair bit of practice with that, forming a VMI (Vivid Mental Image) when you were creating your archetypes in Chapter Three, and again in Chapter Five. Now we are going to use that same skill to a greater degree.

Visualisation, like all thinking processes, is a function of the physical brain, rather than the mind, which does not exist in a physical sense at all – nobody has so far been able to categorise exactly what it is. Yet thoughts are controlled by the mind, so the mind and brain together form a magnificently powerful device that can be thought of as an Intelligence Engine.

The logical part of this Intelligence Engine – we will call it the left half, since logic is the domain of the left half of the brain – deals with information one piece at a time, using a high degree of awareness, which makes it rather slow and inefficient sometimes. It functions by reasoning things out, using conscious comparisons and perceived priorities, which can shift by the second as new information comes in. This is where conscious thoughts originate.

The instinctual part – the right half – is extremely complex and can deal with many pieces of information at once, making it very fast in operation. This part of the Engine is concerned with reactions and response, using ancestral memory patterns rather than logical thought. It is the domain of imagery, hunches and instinctive understandings, which can sometimes be amazingly accurate.

There have been many experiments that indicate that the left half of the brain reacts to the activities of the right half, including imagination. This is obviously very important to us; the logical part of our Intelligence Engine is going to attempt to follow the 'requests' from the instinctual part, including things that we simply imagine... or visualise.

This is the facility that we are going to use to achieve the objectives listed at the beginning of this chapter. You *could* do it simply by sitting down in a comfortable place and creating a VMI of exactly how you want to be and what you want to happen... you would need to spend a fair amount of time each day, though, doing just that. This is how most self-help methods work, in fact – with a 'daily routine' that *must* be carried out to ensure success. But you will not need to carry out any daily work at all (though you can if you wish, and have the time and inclination to do so). You can use the methods outlined here just once or twice a week, and they will still work. The only reason we need to do them at all is to get certain processes under way in the first place; they also help to speed things up a bit.

The only essential part of the programme is that you create a VMI of your archetypes as and when you need them, and of your main archetype from time to time, whenever you feel like it or when you have a few seconds – literally – to spare. And even that can cease, once you have modified your fundamental belief system. By then, accessing the attributes you need for any situation in which you find yourself will be an entirely automatic process.

Other Senses

Before we get to the actual *modus operandi*, it is important to recognise that effective visualisation can and should use more senses than just visual imagery. These other senses are all part of the instinctual half of our Intelligence Engine, and everyone has the ability to imagine them at work. That ability can easily be enhanced with practice. Just *imagine* the following sensory stimuli:

Smells	*Sounds*	*Touch Sensations*
Coffee	Dog barking	Animal fur/hair
Garlic	Breaking glass	Sandpaper
Bad eggs	Car crash	Oil/grease
Roses	Aeroplane	Cloth
Petrol	Laughter	Newspaper
Newly cut grass	Pop music	String

You may not be able to 'get' all of these, but you should be able to imagine most of them. Once you have learned the knack, you will soon be able to imagine any smell you have ever experienced, any sound you have ever heard, any texture you have ever felt. If you have truly neglected your imaginative senses, it may be necessary for you to 'tune' them by physical practice – that is, smell things, feel things and listen to things – and think about them.

Methods

The major advantage of the methods shown here is that they make it easy to create a VMI that is more detailed and specific than one you would create in 'waking' life. It will be effective with the simple concentration enhancer, but many times more so using the self- hypnosis routine. Before you start, though, decide which particular objective you are going to work at. You *can* work on more than one, but then your energies will be spread more thinly; you will generally get results more quickly if you narrow your area of concentration. In a minute, we will have a look at one example of each of the three objectives.

First, find a comfortable place to sit, where you can be undisturbed for as long as you need. Twenty minutes or so is sufficient for most people, though some like to take longer, especially at the beginning. During this time, set aside any non-urgent problems that may need to be dealt with later in the day. This will be easier if you remember a few points:

1.   The problem is transient, as all problems are.

2.   You could not change it any way even if you *did* keep it in your mind during this short time.

3.   You will be able to deal with it more easily and efficiently afterwards as a result of the mental imagery work that you are about to do.

Many people find it helpful to visualise a box in which they place all their mental and emotional 'rubbish', to keep it safe for a short while so that they can use all their energies in the most efficient manner possible.

Having mentally cleared your mind, go through either a self-hypnosis routine (shown in Chapter Eight) or the concentration enhancer; once you are ready, create a VMI of whatever you have decided to work on, *making certain to use as many of your senses as you can.* For maximum effectiveness, this VMI will be animated, looking, smelling, sounding and feeling as much like real life as you can get it! You can think of it as an 'action VMI' of you behaving as you would like to behave, looking exactly as you would like to, and feeling as you would want to actually feel.

Suppose for a moment that you have decided to develop the positive aspects of your major personality type. An effective way to tackle this is to remember the short descriptions given in Chapter Five: Forceful, Resolute, Organisational for the Warrior; Sociable, Intuitive and Adaptable for the Settler; Restless, Charismatic and Innovative for the Nomad. The action VMI you create should be of any situation that can embody any or all of the relevant attributes – it will be even more effective you base it on a real life experience, visualising the outcome exactly the way you want it to be. Make sure, though, that you are accessing a situation where your major group could have achieved good results.

Now we will look at something different. This time let's assume that you are working on your fundamental belief system. You have a choice here. You can either just let your mind drift through the concepts expressed in the passages you made a note of in Chapter Six, when images that can be developed may present themselves to you without any effort on your part at all; you can create a relevant action VMI; or you can recall a time or times in the past when your fundamental belief system has caused problems. In this case, of course, you will create an action VMI of success.

Attributes and Affirmations

Now we will look at how to develop the attributes you have listed as a result of the conflicts revealed in Chapter Four. Here, the best way is to use what are known as *affirmations*. Affirmations are simply short phrases which you repeat to yourself, aloud if possible, over and again – say, ten times each. You will often find an image accompanying these affirmations, or even a memory of a time when that attribute was needed, in which case you could work with it as shown above. You can write your own affirmations, making certain that they are phrased positively, or you can use any on this list that are relevant. They are all written in such a way as to be totally acceptable to the personality group from which they originate.

Reliability

I am steady, stable and reliable, and will remain so for the rest of my life.

I am forthright, trustworthy and honest in all my dealings.

Spontaneity

I make decisions quickly, and my decisions are correct because of this.

My spontaneity assures me of a full, active and enjoyable life.

Inspirational

My way of being inspires and impresses others.

I achieve amazing results with everything I do.

Adaptability

I am adaptable, and my adaptability assures me of success.

I am a natural optimist; I can always turn a setback into an advantage.

Shrewdness

I am perceptive and shrewd, and my shrewdness pleases me.

I quickly see and use all opportunities for success.

Determination

I am always determined and will always remain so.

I am tenacious and persevere with all my efforts towards success.

Whether you are using an action VMI, a memory, or an affirmation, always remember to use as many senses as you can, as vividly as you can. It is a little more difficult to employ senses with affirmations than it is with a VMI, but it is *only* difficult...

Reward Yourself

An important aspect of this work is the psychological reward in the form of emotion; whatever you visualise, imagine yourself receiving gratification of some sort at the moment of success. You could see an image of yourself looking victorious, jubilant,

over-the-moon, radiant, exultant, triumphant, elated, ecstatic –
however you feel when something really good happens. See yourself punching the air, cheering, receiving applause, jumping for
joy... vividly imagine how it feels when these things actually happen, and let it make you feel good!

The natural human drive towards pleasure will motivate your
subconscious to find exactly what you want; simple 'cold'
visualisation, without the joyous emotion is unlikely to work as
effectively.

Concentration and Invigoration

You may struggle somewhat at first, but as you get used to the routine, you will probably discover that you become so engrossed in
visualisation that you 'lose yourself' until you have finished. This
is quite normal and is brought about by your improving concentration, a happy side-effect of this sort of work. You might also
notice that you feel invigorated afterwards. Again, this is quite
normal, and brought about by the sense of well-being as you
vividly see yourself looking exactly as you want to be.

Many people want to know how long it will take to effect useful
change; well, some changes have probably become evident
already, but the good news is... it does not actually stop until you
are happy with the way things are, the way you are! It is a gradual
and continuous process, because as you access your ancestral
archetypes, you keep strengthening the resources that you have
inherited.

Psycho Morphing

Psycho morphing – the name comes from the video morphing
sometimes used in TV advertising to change one image seamless-
ly into something totally different – is a kind of blending technique
whereby you can access exactly the right balance between two different personality groups when you cannot make your mind up
about which archetype would be the best for a particular situation.

It relies on a certain amount of instinctive 'feel' and may not work well for everybody straightaway; in some instances it might not work at all. It is offered here simply as another tool, ideal for those occasions where it is important that you 'get it right' and where you have some advance notice.

Let us assume, for a moment, that you have to deal with a situation that seems to demand the communicative skills of the Settler but in which you are having to negotiate with somebody whom you know to be a Warrior type. What you need is obviously somewhere between the two, and you can 'morph' between them until it feels right for you. Another way of looking at it is that you are going to retain as much of your major group as you can whilst using as much of the other as you need.

To produce what you want, create a VMI of both archetypes on opposite sides of your field of vision. Now, halfway between them, visualise a new character, a composite that is somewhere between the two extremes (it is the ability to do this which is necessary for this technique to work). Get the 'feel' of this composite character. If you need more Warrior than now exists, then create another composite midway between the new one and the Warrior; if you need more Settler attributes, then work on that side. When you have what you want, 'lock' that image into your mind for access when you need it.

If you find you simply do not have the 'feel' required to do this (most Nomads will, and many Settlers, but fewer Warriors), then you will need to rely on the ability to switch between archetypes as necessary; the technique for that is covered later.

What Can it Do?

Used wisely, visualisation techniques can enhance your whole life. Here are just a few immensely useful applications:

1.   Put non-urgent problems 'on hold' for a short while so that you apply your whole attention to more pressing matters. Visualise a strongbox or other safe place where you can

mentally store them in a symbolic form (a slip of paper or a lead weight, for example – it doesn't matter what). See yourself placing the problem into the box and slamming the door shut, knowing that it is safe to leave it there unattended until you want to return to it later. You will often be surprised that when you do so, there is a solution with it!

2. Think yourself well – literally visualise yourself bursting with health and vitality, making it truly vivid in your mind. This can help to keep your immune system in tiptop condition.

3. Increase your energy levels – see yourself as if on film, or standing outside yourself, simply bursting with energy and well-being.

4. Visualise yourself dealing easily with situations and circumstances that concern you – speaking in public, for example. There is a special, very powerful method for this, the 'Swish' technique, described in full at the end of this chapter.

Visualisation can help you excel in just about anything you want to. All you have to do is imagine yourself in the appropriate mode, looking exactly as you want to feel, behaving exactly as you want to behave – and succeeding.

It is interesting that, thousands of years ago, our ancestors were using the selfsame process that you are learning here. On the walls of their caves, they drew scenes of what they wanted to happen – success in hunting, success in battle, and so on. Once dismissed by 'experts' as primitive 'sympathetic magic', it is likely that these ancestors of ours actually realised the power of 'mind rehearsal' to help along the things that they wanted to happen. Nowadays, it is a firmly held psychological principle that what you rehearse in your mind is more readily available to you in real life, and visualisation coupled with deep relaxation or hypnosis is perhaps the most effective form of mind rehearsal that is available to us.

A Case History

Change can sometimes be very subtle, and you may not even believe that it has anything to do with this process when it happens, because it feels so natural. At first, you may not even be aware that these changes have taken place.

One man had been working with a professional therapist for a few weeks, using visualisation to seek career enhancement (there is more about specific goals later on), when he reported dejectedly: "I'd set my heart on getting the next promotion at work. I've been feeling really good about it and I was absolutely certain that it would come my way – but it didn't. A real plodder got it instead. So it hasn't worked, and I feel like it's all pointless – a complete waste of time."

His disappointment was understandable: his personality assessment had revealed a strong Warrior trait heavily imprinted with Settler behaviour patterns with which he had always felt uncomfortable. A few sessions of addressing fundamental beliefs, resolving subconscious conflicts and strengthening his Warrior attributes had resulted in a far more positive and confident way of being. And now, apparently, it was all to no avail.

The therapist's advice was to keep doing what he had been doing, because he would still get what he wanted. He was a bit doubtful, but agreed to carry on; only a fortnight later, he discovered that a new department was being set up and he had been appointed manager! Apparently, he *had* been considered for the original promotion, but his bosses (at a major international company) had decided that his positive manner would be of more use to the company in a managerial position.

Of course, had his improvement been less profound, he would probably have got the job he first went for – and would have felt successful!

Negative Self-Influence

We have one other important area to deal with via visualisation before we can continue – the area of negative self-influence. This can have been created by somebody from your formative years (a schoolteacher, neighbour, family 'friend', etc.) who made you feel consciously awkward; it can be the result of comparing yourself unfavourably with somebody who you viewed as being almost perfect; it can even come from some negativity towards one of the archetypes that you yourself have created. Apart from this last reason, the events or people concerned are in your past and no longer important, since everything in your present life will shift as you work on your fundamental belief system.

We will tackle the archetype and 'real person' situations separately – the 'real person' situation first. The concentration enhancer will be perfectly adequate for this exercise, though you can use self-hypnosis if you prefer.

Create a VMI of the individual to whom you are attributing negative influences with him or her behaving in the way that caused the problem. You may have to work at this in the same way that you had to work to recall negative memories in Chapter Six, but don't allow yourself to be satisfied with the belief that it was *everything* this person did – there will always be one aspect of his or her behaviour that is a focal point. If it was a teacher, for example, you might remember being subjected to humiliation or shouting, or some other sort of punishment or negative treatment. If it was a relative, then you may well remember the same sort of thing – or worse... (Never shy away from unpleasant memories. Working through them can only relieve you of the associated stress.)

Having created your VMI, visualise which mode you would adopt as an adult to handle that situation, and create another VMI – a VMI of you doing just that, but doing it in a legal manner, efficiently and fairly. Repeat the process until you are bored with it, using several different events if you feel the need.

Then let it go.

Recognise an important fact: the best way for you to feel comfortable and at ease within yourself is to simply let go of the negative associations. "Easier said than done!" you might want to reply. Well, that is only true if you make it so. If you want to hang on to hate, jealousy, anger or whatever because you do not see why you should 'let somebody off', then that is obviously entirely up to you. It will make no difference to the object of your negativity, but it *will* severely diminish your own chances of happiness or success. How can you be happy with negative feelings inside you?

Nothing can be 'unhappened', no matter what course of action you take. Even punishing the individual involved cannot change what has already occured, and though you may believe it would make you feel better, all the evidence points to the reverse effect – negative emotions actually increase.

As long as you hold on to negative emotions, you are effectively giving that person – who has already caused you problems once – power to affect the way you feel, power to spoil your life.

Let it go – and feel good!

Negativity from Archetypes

Any negativity that you feel about any of your archetypes is nothing more than a projection of how you would feel if you came face to face with that individual in real life – so a Settler, for instance, might be anxious about the idea of coming face to face with the Warrior; the Warrior, in turn, might feel that the Settler's conscientious way of being is an exhibition of some sort of weakness. Well... relax. The archetypes are totally under your control, because they are dependent upon you for their very existence! Your major personality group will always be dominant, even when being influenced by one of the others.

The Warrior will *use and control* the attributes of the Settler or Nomad.

The Settler will *adapt and modify* the attitudes of the Nomad or Warrior.

The Nomad will *act the part* of the Warrior or Settler.

It works!

The 'Swish' Technique

The Swish technique is from a branch of psychology known as NLP (Neuro-Linguistic Programming) and is used for a great many purposes by successful people all over the world. There are many situations in which it can be useful, but it is particularly suitable for helping you deal with one-off situations where you need a confidence boost.

To use it successfully, you need to be in a comfortable place where you will not be disturbed. It is best if you are wide awake – you will have your eyes closed, and if you are tired, it is easy to fall asleep because of the technique's somewhat repetitive nature. It can be used with self-hypnosis for extra effectiveness.

Sit or lie comfortably and close your eyes. Steady your breathing and relax your body as much as you can for a minute or two; play some favourite music if you find this helps. Now create, in your mind's eye, a VMI of you just at the moment of having to deal with the anxiety-causing situation. It must be as vivid and sharp as you can make it, filling your whole vision, the colours bright and alive, with you looking just as uncomfortable as you can possibly imagine. Make it seem like an enormous colour slide being projected in your mind, and include anything that will make it more lifelike: other people around you, their expressions, the scenery, sounds, smell, touch, etc. – anything. It can be a short action VMI if you like. When it is vivid enough that it actually makes you squirm, then you have got it right. We will call that VMI the 'moment of anxiety'. Giving it a name makes it easy for you to recall later on, but for now, just put it to one side in your mind.

Now for something more comfortable. This time you are going to create a VMI (again, a short action scene if you prefer it) of you in the right mode for the task, just at the moment when you have successfully dealt with the problem. Again, make it as vivid as is humanly possible and use the same techniques as before to make it truly lifelike. We will call this one the 'moment of achievement'. In it, you should be looking exactly as if you have just been incredibly successful with the specific circumstance. When you get it right, when it makes you feel good, allow yourself to enjoy it for a moment. Then imagine it shrinking, becoming smaller and smaller, with the colours fading, until you are left with a small black-and-white picture the size of a postage stamp. Then lay it to one side in your mind, just as you did the first one. Now:

1. Pick up the 'moment of anxiety' VMI, and make sure it fills your entire vision – just as sharp, just as lifelike, just as 'squirm-making' as it was before, but with an important addition: the small, black-and-white 'moment of achievement' image is tucked into the bottom left-hand corner.

2. When you have that image clearly in your mind, just say to yourself: "S-W-I-S-H", at the same time changing the pictures over in your mind so that the 'moment of achievement' becomes the large colour picture and the 'moment of anxiety' fades to black and white and shrinks to the size of a postage stamp tucked into the bottom left-hand corner.

3. Enjoy it for just a few moments.

4. Let your mind drift to some neutral place. This can be anywhere you like – a room in your house, the park, a deserted beach, anywhere, as long as it is a place where you are comfortable and at ease. It is very important that you make this switch to a neutral place each time; once again, it can be a short action VMI or a 'still'.

Now start again at Step 1 and continue to repeat the sequence. After a while, you will find that the pictures change over so easily and so rapidly that you scarcely have any time to see the 'moment of anxiety' before it is replaced with the 'moment of achievement'. This can take as few as three or four attempts. This should be repeated every day, until the pictures change instantly right from the start, or you find that you cannot produce the 'moment of anxiety' picture at all.

When that happens, you have programmed yourself for success rather than failure. You will find that when you actually get to the event you have been working on, you will feel confident and easy, and able to give your best. It might all sound rather complicated at first, but you will soon get used to it and it is worth persevering with. It is one of the most powerful 'quick-fix' methods in existence.

For an example, we will use driving test fear. The moment of anxiety would be, perhaps, sitting in the car – looking very anxious, perhaps having trouble with the seat belt, the examiner looking stern. The feeling of 'nerves' could be included, too. The moment of achievement could be: confident Settler mode, tearing up the L-plates, big smile, congratulations from the examiner, a feeling of excitement and jubilation. Maybe even a congratulatory pat on the back from a friend. In these images, anything goes, as long as they give you absolutely the right feeling, both the anxiety and the jubilation. The neutral place could be simply relaxing in front of the television.

The 'Swish' technique can help you excel in exams and other test situations, at public speaking, sports – in fact, *any* situation where you can create those two pictures.

Chapter Eight
Hypnosis
and Self-Hypnosis

Some people are anxious about hypnosis and self-hypnosis and would vigorously resist the idea of using it. It is not an essential part of the self therapy outlined in this book, and you may comfortably rely on the use of the concentration enhancing routine shown in Chapter Three instead. But even if you decide on that course, it is a good idea to at least read through this chapter, as it will give you a clearer insight into this unique phenomenon, which is surrounded by far too many myths and misconceptions.

Hypnosis, viewed with suspicion by many, is not magical or mystical; it does not make anybody superhuman, nor does it endow an individual with mystical powers beyond the understanding of the normal human mind. Nor does it cause anybody to 'burn up resources' for which there is an eventual price to be paid. It is nothing more than a psychological tool – and an amazingly efficient one – that can help anybody who chooses to use it to achieve excellence.

The ancient Greeks used a form of it several thousand years ago, so it is hardly a modern fad (it is virtually certain that those ancient ancestors of ours would have used one or more of its many forms – all magical rites can technically be considered to be a form of hypnosis as also, to an extent, can religious ritual). 'Hypnosis' is a relatively modern name for it, though, coined in 1841 by James Braid, a Scottish surgeon of high reputation who made the first scientific investigation of the phenomenon. Misunderstanding the condition at first, he named it after *Hypnos*, the Greek god of sleep. Later, when he realised that there was no sleep state of any kind involved, he wanted to change it. But he was too late; the name had grabbed the imagination of the public and was here to stay.

There are many people who believe hypnosis to be 'weird', dangerous, risky to the mentality, or in some other way potentially harmful, so we will spend a little time examining the true nature of the phenomenon. You may find yourself questioning some of the following statements, since they go completely against popular belief and myth, and even some newspaper reports; any professional hypnotist or hypnotherapist, though, would confirm their truth.

◆ *You cannot get 'stuck' in hypnosis – this is quite impossible.*

◆ *You do not become in any way unconscious or semi-conscious.*

◆ *You cannot, at any time, be made to do things you do not want to do.*

◆ *You are totally aware of yourself and your surroundings at all times.*

◆ *You do not go to sleep – you do not even have to have your eyes closed.*

◆ *You are not in anybody's power, and nobody can take control of you.*

◆ *You can voluntarily leave the hypnotic state whenever you wish to.*

◆ *You cannot 'leave your body'.*

◆ *You cannot 'lose your mind'.*

◆ *You cannot be 'possessed' in some way.*

◆ *Hypnosis is a truly natural state of mind and body.*

◆ *There is no such thing as a 'hypnotised feeling'.*

Strong Minds do it Better...

Almost everybody can be hypnotised – the only exceptions are very young children, alcoholics or individuals under the influence of alcohol, some hard drug addicts, and those with learning difficulties. The ability to enter the hypnotic state is linked to intelligence and creativity; therefore those with a 'strong mind' will be particularly capable of using this amazing facet of their own psyche, as long as they actually *want* to be hypnotised.

Being 'unhypnotisable' would certainly be nothing to boast about, because it would show a distinct weakness of mental faculties. There is no special strength involved in resisting it, because *anybody* can resist it, simply by deciding that they are not going to be hypnotised.

One of the sources of misconceptions about this phenomena is the type of film or TV programme where a hypnotised person is shown getting up to all sorts of things without remembering it afterwards. Usually, someone mutters a trigger word in their presence, and off they go into a glassy-eyed funny walk, performing whatever they are asked to do or programmed to perform; they cannot be brought out of it until somebody says the 'antidote' word. This is all very convenient for writers, but based purely on their own misconceptions, which they have learned from the writing of others. When you see such a thing you can be sure that there has been virtually no research (or any research has been ignored) as to the validity of the scene. Sometimes hypnosis is depicted the way it is because the real thing looks so normal it would be boring for the viewer!

The Trigger Principle

Trigger words sometimes are used by professional therapists to help individuals do something they already want to do but may have been finding difficult – quitting smoking, for example, or feeling more confident when meeting people or speaking in public. But a trigger word works only if the 'subject' wants it to – the individual will not do anything he or she does not already want to. And there is no need for an 'antidote' to release the person from a trance afterwards, because no trance occurs in the first place. The trigger is simply a reminder to the subconscious of the desired outcome of a situation.

It *is* possible to use a pre-designated trigger word (that has been suggested during a previous session) to induce hypnosis, but again, it only works if the subject wants it to. It may also be reassuring to know that if, at any time in hypnosis, any sort of emergency should arise or anything needed your attention, you would simply leave the hypnotic state instantly and deal with the situation just as you would have done normally. Well, actually, that's not quite accurate; you would probably deal with that situation *far more easily* than you would otherwise have done.

To put all the above into a nutshell – you and you alone are in control of your own hypnotic state.

Popular Ideas

Let's take a brief look at some misrepresentations of hypnosis.

The stage show

The stage hypnotist uses his skills to quickly pick out, from among his volunteers, those who will be happy to go along with everything he asks them to do – the eager ones who are practically bursting to be in on the act. It's not that the others *cannot* be hypnotised, it's just that he prefers to work with the easy, willing ones – and why not? This *is* entertainment, whether you agree with it or not.

The stage hypnotist is a master at harnessing the power of suggestion, just as a stage magician is. And if you doubt the power of suggestion, then just think about the times that you have made an enthusiastic purchase after reading or seeing an advertisement, or even a window display, only to discover that that the product is not quite as you had imagined it would be. That advertisement relied on the power of suggestion to get you to believe that the product was just what you wanted. Most of the 'tricks' you see performed on stage are the result of manipulation of the power of suggestion.

Most of the stage volunteers, if you were to ask them afterwards, would confide that they had not 'gone under', that they were not hypnotised. But they would believe that everybody else was.

The swinging pendulum

In films, especially old ones, hypnosis is often shown being induced by a swinging pendulum or some other form of eye fixation. Actually, these are just two of the very many methods of inducing hypnosis, and although they work quite well, they are seldom used these days because they are slow and often ineffective. Most modern therapists use just their voice and work with the relaxation methods (or similar) described for self-hypnosis later in this chapter.

Hypnotic amnesia

Many people believe that you cannot remember anything that happens while you are hypnotised. That, though, is just another myth; people usually remember as much as, or more than, they would have done without hypnosis. The only exceptions here are where the conscious mind has wandered off into the realms of imaginative thought in the same way that it can sometimes do while you're watching TV; or where there has been a specific suggestion for amnesia. In the latter case, the amnesia would only last until there was some sort of reminder of what had transpired throughout the session.

'Going under' and coming up again

You do not feel as if you 'go under' any time during hypnosis, because there is actually no such thing as a hypnotised feeling. In self-hypnosis, you can simply decide that your eyes will open after, say, twenty-five minutes, and that is exactly what will happen. If somebody were to hypnotise you and then leave you to your own devices, then you would simply leave the state yourself.

Self-Hypnosis

It really is very easy to hypnotise yourself, though because there is no such thing as a hypnotised feeling, you will probably not, at first, recognise it when you get there. It is almost inevitable that you will believe that it has not worked for you – and even more inevitable that it will. That is, if you want it to and allow it to.

Hypnosis itself will do nothing for you because, as stated at the beginning of this chapter, it is simply a tool. The very best wood-working tools in the world will not produce a single stick of furniture until they are properly used by somebody who has learned what to do with them. It is what you do within the state of hypnosis that is important – the tasks of imagination and imagery that are clearly described within the pages of this book. Anything that can be done with the concentration enhancer can be done super-efficiently with self-hypnosis.

Now, we will look at how you can best induce hypnosis within yourself.

A Warning

First, though, a warning: do not expect to find anything exciting happening. In fact, like most people when they first discover what hypnosis actually is, you will probably either not believe that it is 'proper' hypnosis, or you might decide that it cannot possibly live up to the claims made for it, because it seems so ordinary and commonplace. Well, it most certainly is 'proper' hypnosis, as used professionally on a daily basis by many thousands of practising hypnotherapists throughout the world. Even where different methods (and there are many) of inducing this pleasant state are used, the hypnosis is still the same. Hypnosis is hypnosis. Some people go into a deep state, others only a light one, but that is no more important than that some people are light sleepers while others happily snore through thunderstorms.

Three Methods

Three effective methods of inducing self-hypnosis will be described here. The first, most pleasant, and by far the longest, is *guaranteed* to hypnotise absolutely *everybody* who can be hypnotised. It is advisable to use this method for your first few attempts, because in addition to being the longest – it takes about fifteen minutes or so, if you do it at the right pace – it is the most reliable, and you can learn from it exactly how hypnosis seems to you. Even though there is no such thing as a hypnotised *feeling*, there *are* certain 'signs' that hypnosis is present, and we will have a look at these later on.

The second method is one that you may be able to use immediately, especially if you have a particularly good imagination and an actively creative mind (Nomads are usually *excellent* at this one); the third method is for 'experts' only! It is very swift, and not everybody is able to use it.

Method one – relaxation and deepener technique

This might seem a lot to remember at first, and you will need to read through the routine a few times before you can begin to practice – and like all skills, this will need practice. Of course, you do not have to learn it word-for-word, merely the concept of what you have to do and how you have to do it. You could even record it onto tape, reading in a slow, steady, soothing voice, then use it to produce the hypnotised state. You will notice that there is little punctuation in the relaxation and deepener section of the script, though there are frequent small pauses – this is to produce an even flow of words and ideas.

In many ways, it is better to take the time to learn it well enough so that you do not have to rely on anything but the power of your own mind. When you are proficient, you will probably choose to start with your eyes closed, but it is a good idea to practise the routine even as you read it for the first time. Do not go too fast; it is all about allowing yourself to become steadily more relaxed as you go through it. It is a good idea to sit in a comfortable chair, rather than lie down, because it is *so* relaxing that it is all to easy to drift off to sleep.

The preparation

1.   Make yourself comfortable, place your feet flat on the floor and just let your hands lie loosely in your lap. Allow yourself to feel lazy; if you are sitting upright, let your head fall forward, rather than back, as you relax.

2.   Close your eyes now. (OR fix your eyes on a single point somewhere in the room and stare at it, allowing your eyes to close naturally when they want to; it does not matter how long this takes.) Relax your eyes and eyelids to the point where you simply cannot be bothered to even try to open them, even though you know you easily could. Steady your breathing, breathing evenly and easily, making sure that each breath takes the same amount of time as the one before it and the one after it. Saying "R-e-l-a-a-x" to yourself with each breath out will help this preparation stage.

3.   After five or six breaths, start to count from 1 to 10 in your mind, slowing down as you get closer to 10. It's not necessary to go too slowly here – about 20 seconds or so overall is about right. As you count, imagine yourself becoming lazier with each number; imagine yourself going into a wonderful, relaxed sort of feeling where you have nothing whatsoever to do except to relax. (You might already have started to notice some small physical changes occurring in your body, all associated with relaxation. If not, you are probably trying too hard – all you have to do is... nothing.)

Relaxation

This is probably the most important part of the routine, especially at first, and must not be overlooked.

Think about the top of your head, because many people don't realise that tension often starts in the little muscles of the scalp... so think about those little muscles and the skin of your scalp and just allow them to let go and relax... now think of your forehead, allowing it to smooth out and relax... actually feel the skin settling and smoothing out... and the muscles around your eyes and eyelids now... just let those muscles let go... and the rest of your face, the cheeks, mouth and jaw muscles, just letting all those areas go slack and relax... it's a beautiful feeling when you can let your face totally relax like this, because you can actually feel tension draining away from you like a fluid... this might mean that your mouth opens slightly, but whatever feels most comfortable to you... just let it happen... unclenching your teeth and relaxing your tongue, because the more you physically relax, the more you can mentally relax... so that soon you can discover for yourself that wonderful, super-relaxed state called hypnosis... when your eyes are closed, you might feel them flickering from side to side as you relax... or you may notice that your eyelids want to open just slightly, or maybe feel them fluttering or quivering... these are all early signs of hypnosis, but it doesn't matter if you don't feel any of these sensations... because you'll enter hypnosis just as easily and then you'll be more relaxed than you can ever imagine... now think about your neck and shoulder muscles and the tops of your arms... just as though you were sending out a wave of thought... that relaxes each muscle, each cell, each fibre of your whole body as it goes... so that as you think on down through your elbows... into your forearms... you can feel all those areas relaxing, too... down through your wrists... now into your hands... right the way down into your fingers and thumbs... into the very tips of your fingers and thumbs... just letting all those muscles be beautifully relaxed and easy... very lazy... think about your breathing now... noticing that you're breathing more steadily, more slowly, as you relax more and more, so you can let any tension in the chest area simply drain away as you think on down to the muscles of the abdomen, letting those muscles relax, too... think about your back now, the long muscles either side of the spine, just let those muscles relax, and your waist... and your buttocks... now just relaxing the anus and genital areas... so that you are beginning to feel very comfortable now... maybe noticing that you are starting to feel heavier with each breath you breathe... now relaxing your main thigh muscles as you think on down through your knees... down through the shins and calves, just allowing all those areas to relax and let go, as you think about your ankles... down through your feet, right the way down into the very tips of your toes... all the muscles of your body beautifully relaxed and easy... feeling very lazy now, and comfortable... beginning to become aware of the weight of your arms, the weight of your legs... maybe even beginning to feel that super-relaxed sensation as if your whole body is becoming... heavier and heavier... with each breath you breathe, a wonderful sensation of total physical relaxation.

The deepener

This is the most variable part of any hypnotic induction. It is used to deepen the state of hypnosis that by now already exists, (even though you are probably unaware of it.) Again, it is not necessary to know it off by heart; it is the general concept that matters, and making everything as vivid as you can in your mind, or, of course, you can record it.

Staying perfectly relaxed with your eyes closed, imagine yourself standing on the very top of a green hill on a tropical island... you can feel the warmth of the sun on your head and shoulders and can see the long grass around you moving slightly in the gentlest of breezes... when you look down the hill you can see a narrow, winding path that disappears into a small forest.. and beyond the forest you can see the ocean... with sunlight from the clearest of blue skies glancing off the tops of the waves in the bay... so that the whole ocean seems to shimmer and sparkle... you begin to move lazily and easily down the path, with the ferns and grasses brushing gently against your legs as you pass... and you just catch the faint smell of salt borne in on the breeze and become aware of the distant sound of the ocean on the shore... maybe hear seabirds calling faintly, from a long way off...

You marvel at the deep sense of calmness and tranquillity that sweeps over you, as you move on down and down towards the forest... moving so easily, so effortlessly, you feel almost as though you're floating on air... and in no time at all you find yourself drifting through the trees, their leaves closing overhead to form a canopy... their branches making an irregular pattern against the clear blue of the sky. It's pleasantly cool in the forest, and the gentle sound of birds singing, echoing faintly, and the scent of the trees and undergrowth relaxes you still further... as you move easily into the inviting depths, becoming lazier and lazier with each step you take... you can hear a stream somewhere, its gurgling sound gradually mingling with the sound of the ocean... as you follow the winding path down and down towards the beach that you know is in front of you, weaving through the trees and brushing aside the occasional piece of foliage... until, quite suddenly... you feel the welcoming warmth of the sun on your head and shoulders again and you find yourself on a beautiful deserted beach... a beautiful golden shoreline sweeping away in a gentle curve in front of you, to a distant point where the trees seem to come right down to the shoreline, so that their branches actually seem to overhang the ocean itself.

You can feel the sand warm between your toes as you stroll lazily across the broad beach to the water's edge... the sand becomes a darker golden colour when you get there, and you enjoy the change to a moist, firm coolness beneath your feet as you wander along the shore, leaving a lazy trail of footprints in the sand behind you... every so often a larger-than-usual wave sends rivulets of water foaming around your feet... and as they recede, you notice how the sand is washed away from tiny coloured pebbles, glinting like jewels in the sun... the smell of the ocean, the sunlight on the waves, the sound of the water hissing over the sand... all these things seem to make time and space seem less important for some unknown reason... and you find yourself a comfortable position, a grassy hollow maybe, to just sit and gaze out across the rolling depths to the horizon... trickling warm, golden sand idly through your fingers...

There's a faint haze that makes it difficult for you to see exactly where the sky stops and the ocean starts... and as you try to fathom it out, you see a small white cloud appear from somewhere near the horizon... it comes towards the island quite quickly, growing larger as it approaches, until it's immediately overhead... the largest, fluffiest, whitest cloud you can ever remember seeing... and you somehow know, just by instinct, that you can let all your worries, all your cares, all your fears, just drift up towards this large white cloud... you can actually see them drifting away from you in a long slow spiral... maybe like smoke from a bonfire... just spiralling away from you towards this large white cloud... the cloud absorbs all your worries into itself, swallowing up all your fears and anxieties and becoming steadily darker all the time, until, just as it reaches its darkest, just as the last part of that spiral of your worries and cares disappears inside it... the sun bursts through... dispelling every one of your worries, every one of your fears and anxieties, to the edges of the universe... leaving you totally relaxed and perfectly at ease with yourself, without a single care in the world...

And now, all your troubles and cares having floated away from you, you settle yourself down into a comfortable position and just drift off into a deep and relaxing sleep... and while you sleep, you have a dream... you dream you're walking down a long corridor, stretching away in front of you in a long, gentle curve... so long that you can't actually see the end of it... but you know that this corridor is in the very depths of your subconscious mind... in the part of your mind that knows just what to do and just how to do it... and as you begin to move along this beautiful corridor, becoming even more relaxed, even more lazy, you realise that time and space are beginning to lose their meaning... and slowly the walls of the corridor seem to dissolve, leaving you in a large room... the room is full of a gentle golden light that relaxes you still further, and you suddenly realise, with a surge of inspiration and pleasure... that what you once saw as limits are merely stepping stones to greater success... it suddenly dawns on you, with a surge of joy and anticipation, that what once seemed to you to be the limits of your personality, of your skills and abilities, are nothing more than stepping stones to even greater success...

One wall of this room is like a huge television screen with words and images flashing across it too fast for you to see... and you realise that this is information being transmitted to different parts of your mind and body... you use your mind to will it to stop, and as you do so, the screen clears and the word 'READY' appears in large flashing letters...

This is the point at which you will be ready to start the actual psychological work that you need to do.

That particular deepener is very effective, but you do not *have* to use that exact scenario. You can invent your own by simply letting your mind drift through a series of scenes, making them as vivid as you can so that they absorb you completely. They do not have to be logical or even rational, and can be literally anything that makes you feel good... floating lazily down a river in a small boat, under branches of willow trees, listening to the sounds of the water lapping against the sides... maybe floating into a cave, at the far end of which there is a circle of light, through which you drift, to find yourself on a deserted golden beach stretching away into the distance... Or maybe finding yourself floating in a magical rainbow in which time and space are not the same as we usually think of them... Maybe you can drift forwards in time, or back in time, before floating down through the rainbow to a beautiful tranquil lake, which constantly changes colour from a softly limpid blue, to a relaxing, translucent green, before becoming a deep, soft indigo, as you wander lazily along the sandy shore, noticing the scents of the flowering shrubs and feeling soft grasses and ferns brushing against your legs as you pass... There are no rules, and you can allow your imagination free rein to go where it will. Into outer space, if you like, maybe visiting a distant star and observing planet Earth hanging motionless like a great blue and white globe while you are at one with the universe. You can even use variations on the tropical island, perhaps finding ruined cities or abandoned temples with warm spa baths, or maybe gorges within the forest, with paths and steps that take you down into their very depths, where there are magnificent, roaring waterfalls behind which you can go to find caves that lead to wondrous lands where everything is... Well, anyway, you get the idea. A flight of fancy that is a wonderful antidote to that old enemy, stress.

Method two – Imagination and breathing technique

Start with Stage 1 of preparation as for the relaxation and deepener technique, then proceed as follows:

With your eyes closed, imagine, *really* imagine, that you are breathing in through your hands... that your fingers are like hollow tubes and you can actually *feel* the air moving up through your arms and into your shoulders, down through your body and into your legs, and out through your feet. Tell yourself that as the air moves in one single direction through your body, you are breathing calmness into each and every cell, each and every fibre of your entire being... that with each breath out, you are breathing all traces of tension away from you. Let each muscle go limp. As you breath out each time, say to yourself slowly, "R-e-l-a-a-x n-o-w." Keep each breath long, slow and steady, and after six or so imagine that you can feel yourself sinking further and further into the chair with each breath you breathe, that you are steadily becoming more relaxed than you can ever remember. Concentrate on this breathing pattern, breathing in through your hands and out through your feet, until you can actually *feel* yourself sinking. That is when you are in hypnosis, even though the sinking sensation can sometimes be almost immediately replaced with a feeling of extreme lightness.

This routine can produce a good state of hypnosis within just a few minutes and is quite easy to remember. For most people it will work best only after using the longer routine quite a few times first.

Method three – Eye fix, and 'drop' technique

This is probably the most rapid way of getting into hypnosis, but you need to be totally confident and at ease with hypnosis before you can use it effectively. Start with Stage 1 of the preparation technique as before. Then fix your eyes on a single point in the room, preferably above eye level, and stare at it, while concentrating on keeping your breathing slow and even, just as if you were trying to convince someone you were sound asleep. Use the expression "R-e-l-a-a-x   n-o-w" with each breath. After a few moments, you will notice everything around that fixed point begin to become hazy or vague. When that happens, *and not before*, allow your eyes to close, and count slowly down from 10 to 0. At the moment you reach 0, just allow your entire body to 'drop' into relaxation and hypnosis...

Leaving the State

Whichever method you use, you can simply decide to leave this relaxed state whenever you wish, simply opening your eyes and carrying on with your day-to-day business. You can even 'set' your internal timer, telling yourself as you begin your session that you want to leave the hypnotised state after, for instance, half-an-hour. You may be surprised at first, but you will soon get used to how accurate that internal timer is, popping your eyes open just at the time you have requested. Another popular and easy way of leaving hypnosis is to count up to five in your thoughts, after telling yourself that at the count of five, your eyes will open and that you will be wide awake, aware, and feeling good.

Signs

During the state of hypnosis, there are certain bodily reactions, *hypnotic phenomena*, that you will be able to observe when you know what you are looking for. One of the most common is what is known as 'time-distortion', in which your perception of time changes considerably, so that thirty minutes or so may feel like only ten; occasionally it can work in the opposite direction so that it seems more like an hour or even longer. Obviously, this will become apparent only *after* you have finished your session. The following may be noted *during* the session, though they will all disappear the instant you finish.

➤   Your eyes and/or eyelids may flutter, flicker or quiver.

➤   You might feel a small tingling sensation in your facial features.

➤   Your body may feel very heavy, very light or even stiff.

➤   You might feel as if you are gently spinning, or drifting upwards or downwards.

➤   Your mind may be very slow, or very active and alert.

➤   You might feel chilly, as though a door has been left open somewhere.

➤   You might feel as if your whole body has moved or twisted into a totally different position.

➤   Your face may feel warm – there is often a distinct flush to the features during hypnosis.

➤   Your arms and legs may feel as if they have been moved to different positions from how you left them, or may feel 'different' in some other way.

➤   You might experience a tingling sensation like 'pins and needles' in your arms, legs, hands or feet.

There are many other hypnotic phenomena, but these are the most common. You may find yourself experiencing all of them over a period of time, but there will be certain ones that are more frequent. Imagining that those particular phenomena are present when you use the quicker induction techniques is an astonishingly effective way of getting into hypnosis quickly.

With practice, you can choose one of these phenomena to act as a focal point and use it to 'drop' into hypnosis even more quickly than with Method 3. These 'personalised' inductions are very effective, and the majority of professional hypnotherapists use them for themselves on a daily basis.

Now that you know how to induce self-hypnosis, it is a good idea to practise it a few times; after a very short while, you will feel confident enough to use it to help deal with those negative influences – or to help you find success, which is the subject of the next chapter.

Chapter Nine
The Search for Success

Although this chapter will particularly help those who are seeking some form of material success, the 'rules' are pretty much the same for success of any sort. Success is simply the attainment of a goal, and though there is no true 'secret of success' (even though some would have you believe they can teach you one – for a fee, of course) there are four rules that need to be observed if you are to achieve your aims. Those rules are:

➤ The goal must be plausible, possible and realistic.

➤ It must be suitable for your personality type.

➤ You must have a clear idea of what you are seeking.

➤ Positive thinking and positive doing.

Being Realistic

Though the mind is very powerful and can achieve far more than most people realise, any goal you seek must be plausible, possible and realistic. It is no good deciding you want to become a world- class sprinter if you cannot run for toffee! That would be unrealistic. Being able to project your thoughts verbatim into the mind of another person is impossible, so that would not be a good goal, either. And becoming a millionaire in twelve months without lifting a finger is implausible – again, not a viable goal.

But you could decide to join an amateur athletics club and get fit enough to sprint a hundred metres; that is realistic, if you are reasonably able-bodied. And you could set out to become an expert on communications or language – that is certainly possible. Setting up a successful business and becoming your own boss is definitely plausible, though as for becoming a millionaire... well, you might need a little time and a lot of hard work!

In other words, anything that *can* be done, *you* can do. Anything that can *never* be done, you will not achieve. We are not making magic here, we are using natural resources to achieve natural goals.

Suitability

Anything you set out to achieve must be suitable for your personality type if you are to find success *and maintain it afterwards*. The Warrior personality is no more likely to successfully maintain a business where there is a need for tolerance and flexibility, than the Settler – who would probably excel at that job – would do very well in a situation that required emotional detachment and firm control. And a Nomad seeking to become a totally steadfast and calm individual would be about as likely to succeed as a one-legged mountaineer!

Pursuing a dream because it is what you have always wanted is pretty pointless if its demands are outside of the scope of your major personality group. You might achieve something *like* it, and you might achieve some measure of success, but in order to maintain it, you must be a round peg in a round hole.

A Clear Idea

The most important aspect of goal achievement is having a crystal-clear idea of what you want. Without it, you will not know if you are heading in the right direction, nor will you know when you've achieved your goal. It makes no difference whether you are trying to start a successful business or are setting out on a general self-improvement programme – you *must* know where you are going and what you are after.

There are many people who decide that they 'want to make something of themselves', but that is not a goal. It is a simple idea, a concept without any real form. It carries the vague notion that they want to be successful at something but there is absolutely nothing to work at. 'I want to be a better person' is the same sort of thing – nothing clear to work on, no plan to develop. In both those cases, it is impossible to tell which of your archetypes would be best employed to find success, or whether that success would be suitable or likely for you to find. Not only that, both those goals are actually just a fixation on what you do *not* want – they are a look at the way things are and have been, rather than the way you want them to be. The definition of a goal, in this context, is something that you want to achieve in the future.

The person who wants to 'make something' of him or herself is really just stating that their current situation is unsatisfactory. The one who wants to be a better person is saying that they are not happy with the way they are and probably never have been. Later on, those statements will become: "I always wanted to make something of myself… but I never had the chance," or "I didn't choose to end up the way I am. I always wanted to be a better person… but I wasn't given a chance." In both cases, there was only ever one source that the sought-after chance could have come from.

Within. It is where you will find yours.

To access that chance, you need to first write your goal(s) down in as much detail as you possibly can, whether they are for personal improvement, career development, getting a new car, moving to a bigger house in a nicer district, or whatever. A goal can be anything you like, but it must be specific and vividly detailed. Here are a few personality-specific guidelines:

Warrior:

Make sure you focus upon the aspects of the goal that will improve your life and give you specific advantages; maybe it will improve somebody else's life, too, but that is not an issue that will help you find success. Where possible, stay away from areas or ideas where you will have to rely on the support or cooperation of others for success (though there is no problem, of course, in relying on employing others or selling to others). Be sure you find the answers to every perceived snag, every pitfall, before you consider this stage of the process to be complete.

Settler:

Focus on what feels good and seems to fit in with your personal values and moral codes. If what you are planning would cause difficulties for someone else, then resolve that problem before you go any further with your plan. Stay away from areas or ideas where you would be 'out on a limb' and unable to rely on any form of outside resources for help. Fiercely competitive concepts are not for you, either. Be sure to focus on what is right and good about what you want to do, rather than on the 'downside' – trust in your adaptability and ability to solve problems when and if they arise.

Nomad:

Focus on what excites you, enthuses you, 'turns you on'! You love excitement and change, and you will excel at anything that will attract attention and impress or inspire others in some way. Keep away from anything where mundane background work cannot be avoided – or make sure you can delegate those tasks to somebody else – and look for ways in which you can begin to see quick results for your labours. For you, the more noticeable the effects your plan will have, the better your chance of success.

Whichever personality you are, writing your plan down in detail will focus your mind and help to make the eventual VMI you create all the more vivid. Allow yourself as long as it takes (days, if necessary) to create your goal in such detail that it feels almost real, and carries an absolute conviction that it is exactly what you want. When you have got it right, it should easily pass this 'four sense test'. You should be able to create a VMI in which:

1.   You can see it.
2.   You can feel it.
3.   You can hear it.
4.   You can smell it.

Once your goal is achieved, these four senses are what you will enjoy it with – with very few exceptions. Therefore these senses should be able to be activated by your VMI of that goal. Later, we will look at how to make that goal a reality.

Positive Thought

When you have your first three objectives sorted out so that you know what you want and have ensured that it is plausible, possible, realistic, and suitable for your personality type, there is one last but very important rule. It is at least as important as the other three put together, and if you do not take it into account, you will be faced with difficulty at every step.

That rule is to always think in a positive manner.

The concept of positive thinking is astonishingly simple. It just means that you should think of what you *do* want, not what you *do not* want; what you *can* do, not what you *cannot*; what you *like*, not what you *dislike*; how you actually *want* to be, what you actually *want* to happen... etc. For example, "I don't want to look stupid" is a negative statement, whereas "I want to look as if I know what I'm talking about" is positive. By implication, they mean the same thing to the conscious mind, but the subconscious mind does not understand implications.

All of this might sound very obvious, but there are many people who confuse positive with emphatic. "I am *determined* not to fail!" is actually a negative statement, even though it is emphatic, whereas "I am determined to succeed!" is totally positive and carries an entirely different message to your subconscious mind, which is entirely objective and can only work on what actually *is*, and has no understanding of what is *not*.

Another example might help to clarify this. Imagine a small, closed box with a sign on the lid that states '*Inside this box there is not an egg*'. Now imagine another box, identical in every way, except that the sign says '*Inside this box is an egg*'. What object did you think of in the first instance? And in the second? The chances are it was an egg in both instances, because it was the only object that was actually mentioned. So when you state "I am *determined* not to fail," all you will think of is the very thing you *do not* want to happen, the failure... and linked to determination, at that. The only image your subconscious mind will have is the object of the statement, which is exactly the opposite of what you actually meant. In addition to this, it gives your subconscious mind no sense of direction at all, since not failing could mean anything from staying as you are to entering a monastery in order to avoid the risk altogether... Now you can begin to understand why "I am determined to succeed" is so very different.

One of the trickiest negative processes to overcome can be dealing with problems. But it is really quite simple, when you grasp the idea of thinking towards a solution rather than away from the problem. In other words, think towards what you want to happen, rather than just about some way to get away from the problem. The two concepts are, of course, quite different.

Now for a bit of troubleshooting.

Working It Out

Sometimes there seems to be considerable difficulty in setting the goal and thinking about it in a positive enough manner. At other times it simply will not pass that four-sense test – it is as if something in the mind refuses to focus clearly on what you consciously believe you want.

If your difficulty is that you just do not seem to be able to work out exactly what it is you want, then what you are trying to find may not be what you actually want, deep down. This is *diversion*. If, on the other hand, the difficulty is that you know *exactly* what you want, but cannot seem to visualise it very clearly, then you are probably suffering from some form of *resistance*.

Either of these two negative attitudes can be resolved by self-analysis of what motivates or 'unmotivates' you. Resistance is the more difficult of the two situations but can still be overcome, though it may take a little time and a lot of thought. The end result will be worth it.

Diversion Issues

Diversion issues are often easy to recognise and deal with. By far the most common of these is trying to make plans not for what you actually do want, but for what you believe you *should* want. Perhaps you are trying to please somebody else by achieving what they want, or what they insist you should seek, whether their motives are selfish or concerned only with your well-being.

It does not work.

Unless you are working towards what *you* want for yourself, your chances of succeeding are severely limited. Maybe you could motivate yourself to an extent this way, but that motivation will never burn with the same fire as if you are going for something *you* want. Ignore feelings of selfishness, ignore feelings that you owe somebody something, ignore a guilty conscience for any reason at all.

If you are trying to succeed because it would make someone else happy in some way and this is of paramount importance, then it forms part of your plan. But you have to find a goal that will make *you* happy, too, if it is to become a reality. It is not sufficient to simply want to make that other person happy – the drive must come from your mind, not that other person's, so it must be of maximum benefit to you, not somebody else.

If the goal needs money, but money itself does not inspire you, then think about earning that money in a way that will make you feel truly successful. Then make that your goal instead. For instance, if your partner wants to live in a large house but this does not particularly motivate you, then think about being a successful... *anything*... that appeals to you and that would earn enough money to buy the house your partner wants. This has now become an *indirect goal*, something that will take you where you want to go, but by a different route.

Another way of doing it is to merge your goal with the other person's. If, for example, your partner wants that big house, but your goal is a new, luxurious car, imagine yourself in your top-of-the-range limousine, sweeping elegantly through the ornamental double gates of your long gravel drive. Or think of a truly enormous bathroom where you can luxuriate in uninterrupted comfort for hours, contemplating your success and your next move. Or maybe throwing parties for a hundred people or more, where you are the centre of attention. Understanding the attributes of your personality group should give you a clearer idea of how to make your goals more vivid and more readily achievable.

So the indirect goal is something you *can* focus on, which would allow you to automatically achieve some other objective at the same time. Shifting the focus of attention to yourself, to what *you* want, gives you an infinitely higher chance of success. Your subconscious mind will seek out your happiness and yours alone, not someone else's.

Note that for an indirect goal to be effective, there must be no negativity in your mind towards the eventual outcome. So if, for example, you find the idea of making large amounts of money distasteful, you will not override it with an indirect goal; it is a resistance issue.

Diversion can be caused by the goal being set lower than you would really like, possibly because you fear that you may not be able to achieve what you *really* want. Your subconscious will continue to object until you resolve your doubts and make your target what you truly wanted in the first place. Nobody ever became successful by limiting his or her horizons.

Unrealistic resources can also cause doubt. If you need half a million pounds before you can even begin to put your plans into operation, then that amount of money might be an unrealistic resource. Somehow raising it has to become an interim goal in itself. You might, for example, visualise finding venture capital.

There are other forms of diversion, but they all have one thing in common – they are the result of setting goals that are not properly compatible with what you actually want to achieve. Compromise, approximations, better-than-most they may be, but they are not what you really want. Examine those goals in detail and search for the part that does not feel quite right, the part that has some sort of reservation attached or that simply does not fit in with your personality group.

Resistance Issues

Resistance issues are caused by a conflict of interests. What will you do when you have achieved your goal – what will life be like then? If you don't know, have not felt it, dreamt of it, then you simply do not want it badly enough. You have to *really* want the outcome of your plans, absolutely and unconditionally, or there will be a negative thought process at work, deep in the subconscious, that will hinder you. And you have to want *all* of what you will get – the bad bits, if there are any, as well as the good bits. It might seem strange to think that there could be 'bad bits' attached to success. But life is not perfect; it may be that there *is* a 'bad bit' but that it will be far outweighed by the 'good bits'.

For instance, you might consciously be wanting a palatial mansion in the country, while your subconscious is uncertain because you have always grumbled about heating bills in the past. That is a rough-and-ready example, but it serves as an illustration of *conflict*, and conflict is what causes doubt – which is what you are feeling. If you weren't, you would be able to see your image very clearly.

There are always going to be disadvantages, as well as advantages, that come with success, and it is as well to be aware of these. For instance, you might find that some of your friends start to become distant, however close they are now. Your success could make them feel uncomfortable because of their own lack of it, or, if they are already successful in their own right, they might view your success as a threat to their superiority. You may have more money – and more people resenting you for it. You might even find people wondering what sort of 'fiddle' you have discovered! All your protests about working hard and rising by your own efforts are likely to fall on deaf ears, because that is the last thing any detractors will want to hear, let alone accept. It would mean that they would have to admit to inadequacy within themselves.

Bigger houses have bigger bills. Bigger cars use more petrol and have higher repair costs and insurance. Running your own business might mean handling staff efficiently or dealing with awkward customers. There are, of course, many other conflicts of this sort and it is particularly important to recognise that not one of them is insurmountable. Just accepting that they exist and will need to be resolved is often enough to allow those goal images to become clearer in your mind and easier to focus on. And you can always make it an immediate goal to resolve the difficulty in your own mind before you try to progress further.

Making It Work

If your goal does not yet pass that 'four-sense test', it is highly advisable that you identify and work through the problems that are causing that situation. Allowing yourself to be satisfied with the notion that it is simply because you are not very good at visualisation is cheating yourself out of success. You *need* to be good at visualisation in order to create a VMI effective enough to achieve your aims and hopes. All it needs is practice, so read Chapter Seven again, and Appendix 1, until you are at least able to create imagery in all four senses, however vague it might seem. When you have it right, even the least gifted 'visualiser' will be able to do that, even if it is necessary to use each sense individually.

Assuming that you now have a VMI stored in your mind – in action format if necessary – you need to write at least three affirmations associated with it. Though this may take a little time, it is not difficult to do, and it will further focus your mind on your goal. Make sure that each statement is written in a positive manner that could not be misunderstood by anyone. There is a 'golden rule' with a very helpful acronym to remind you of it: KISS. It stands for Keep It Simple, Stupid. In other words, phrase your affirmations as simply and directly as possible. The subconscious *loves* simplicity!

Good starting points are: "I will..."; "I always..."; "I am..."; "I achieve...". Follow these as directly as possible with the object of your goal. For example, "I always... find success." You could add, "Because I expect to find success." Or, this is good: "I will be successful in my attempt to pass my driving test." It could be coupled with "I will feel totally confident when I take my driving test." If there is a specific problem, it can easily be addressed: "I always feel confident in my driving abilities as I approach roundabouts." By now you should have a clear idea of exactly how to phrase your own particular affirmations.

And now the hard work is done!

All you have to do now is apply the visualisation routine described in Chapter Seven, using the VMI and affirmations that you have developed with the help of this chapter. In this case, it is not necessary to access the relevant archetype first (though you can if you want to, of course), since the VMI should have been developed as a result of taking your major attributes into account, and you are – or should be – working at strengthening those attributes already. You can work on these goals at the same time as any 'personal development' work, since it is impossible for there to be any conflict of interests.

Do it every day, without fail, if you can. Your subconscious mind will do the rest, gradually moving you towards the achievement of your goals and aims; it might happen so quickly you hardly have time to draw breath, or it might take so long that you think it is not going to work.

But it will work – and then you can move on to your next goal!

Chapter Ten
Confidence Issues

Of all the psychological problems that affect the human race, at least in the Western world, lack of self-confidence is probably the most common – and the most severely limiting. As with most problems of negative thinking, it usually has its roots in the formative years of childhood, though it is likely that you may not be able to recall anything that accounts for it in any way.

It produces reactions like: feeling stupid, silly or inferior for no real reason; a belief that others see you as stupid, silly or inferior; feelings of embarrassment; a lack of self-esteem or self-worth; fear of other people; fear of new situations; fear of change… and more.

These responses are actually based on an erroneous belief. What is often meant when someone says that they suffer from a lack of self-confidence is that they believe they should be able to do things as easily and confidently as they think other people can, even though there is no way of measuring just how easily or otherwise those other people do perform those tasks. But any comparison you make between how you feel and how someone else looks is invalid, because you cannot assess an internal state from an external appearance – or to put it another way, you cannot judge a book by its cover.

Of course some people *are* more confident overall than others, but the key word is 'some'. They are in the minority. It is actually they who are different to the 'norm'!

Confidence is situation-specific, so someone who feels confident riding a motorbike might well pale at the prospect of getting on a horse, and vice versa. The individual who is anxious about learning to swim may be totally comfortable clambering about on the tenth story of a building under construction. The coal miner who faces the possibility of death every working day might be terrified of speaking in public.

The point is, of course, that in order to deal successfully with personal confidence issues, you need to be specific. You need to work out exactly in which areas of your life you need to be more confident before you can begin to work on self-confidence. There are four common situations, and we will study each of them in some depth:

- Inadequate self-image
- Negative thinking
- Guilt complex
- Inferiority complex

Inadequate Self-Image

Inadequate self-image could be seen as the common root to a great many self-confidence problems, since, more often than not, it results in the belief that your efforts are doomed to failure for no other reason that it is *you* who is making those efforts. It does not matter whether you simply want to make friends more easily, set up and run a successful business, give up a bad habit, start a new hobby, or simply gain enough confidence to stand up and speak in public without blushing or stammering. Whatever it is you want, you find yourself somehow *knowing* that you simply cannot do what other people do... in other words, you expect to fail.

If you expect to fail, then you are looking for failure and will give up at the first sign of it. It is what you were expecting to find, what you were searching for, in fact, so there is no point in continuing your activities. On the other hand, if you expect to succeed, *truly* expect to succeed, then you will continue your endeavours until you do so – because human beings are solution-oriented creatures who continue to search until they find what they are looking for. There is an important saying associated with this process that you should remember:

Be careful what you look for, in case you find it.

If you carry on those same thought processes as you read this book, you will get exactly the same results. You will end up believing that whilst the book might work for other people, it most definitely will not work for you. If this is the case, then you probably have not yet tried any of the techniques shown for self-improvement and are already coming to the conclusion that this is just another one of those things that is designed for the rest of the world.

Well… BOSH!

The first and probably the most important thing to recognise is that having this negative view of yourself is certainly *not* "just the way you are", and there is absolutely no justification for you to continue thinking in this manner. You are not doomed to second-rate results, because you have the instincts and intuitions of your ancestors 'hard-wired' into your psyche. Had their results been second-rate, inferior to others, they would not have survived and you would not be here today, reading this book!

The truth is that you were not born observing yourself in a negative light. It is the result of imprints conditioning you into an erroneous belief about yourself which you have managed to repeatedly reinforce, simply by acting upon it. Maybe you are a Settler with a Warrior parent who has unwittingly led you to believe that you are not tough enough to succeed at anything; maybe, on the other hand, you are a Warrior who has been taught by a Nomad parent that impatience and bluster are the answers to everything… except that you have discovered that they often do not work. If you are not clear about the imprint process, then reread Chapter Six and review your likely conflicts.

The worst thing about the inadequate self-image is that you will readily accept without question the idea that things do not work for you; that you cannot do what you believe other people can do; that you are in some way lacking in some special ability or facility that allows other people to succeed but that guarantees you a life of inadequacy.

But you are not 'special'…neither do you lack anything special that other people have, because that, in itself, would make you special! And since you are not special, 'normal' rules and concepts apply as much to you as they do to anybody else. There is no secret that everybody except you knows, there is no magical power that some people have but which you have been denied – and nobody, including you, is 'doomed to failure'.

That statement is as true if you are trying to achieve a personal goal – gaining personal confidence, for example – as it is if you are trying to set up and run a successful company. Anybody can become successful and realise their goals, as long as those goals are realistic and plausible. The only reason you have not yet done so is because of a belief system that says you cannot. It leads you into making only half-hearted efforts at things you want to achieve, as well as causing you to focus intently on what you do *not* want to happen – making that situation more likely to happen. And the negative belief system is then further reinforced.

The whole problem usually stems from an incongruence between thought and behaviour. It is evidence that your subconscious realises that finding any form of success is going to be unlikely, since you practise in one mode whilst behaving in another. Far from being evidence that you are lacking in some way, it is *proof-positive* that your subconscious is doing a *perfect* job. It is attempting to alert you into mentally rehearsing in the same mode that you usually behave – or behaving in the same mode in which you mentally rehearse. Put briefly, imprints are overriding your natural instinctive behaviour patterns, and your major archetype is being inhibited from working properly.

The work we have already covered in Chapter Six should help to deal with the problem; if it persists, then work further on strengthening the positive attributes associated with your major archetype. Frequent creation of a VMI of 'your' archetype, during self-hypnosis, will greatly accelerate the process.

The Negative Thinker

Most people in this group have, without realising it, been continuously programming themselves for feelings of inadequacy for years and have completely lost sight of all the things that they do without thinking, normal everyday tasks which they do just as well as anybody else. Quite often there are one or two specific situations that cause discomfort, and we will have a detailed look at some of them.

Easily embarrassed

The person who suffers this problem often feels that their ideas and opinions are in some way less worthwhile than those of other people, and that those other people will instantly *know* this to be the case. They might also believe that those other people will know that they feel embarrassed, which embarrasses them even further – this is the syndrome that causes such severe problems for those who blush or stammer, for instance.

The problem can have been caused by a great many things – being ridiculed for perfectly 'normal' things, like having a girlfriend or boyfriend, for example, or trying to learn a new skill; being told that 'you're peculiar', or 'not right'; having your ideas or thoughts laughed at; suffering scorn when trying but failing to do something ordinary; being laughed at in front of others for reasons you did not understand… you get the idea. Isolated instances of any of these things won't do any harm – they are a part of growing up – but if they became such a regular part of your life that you came to expect them and attempted to find ways of avoiding them, then damage was done. They have become imprints and behave like instincts.

Sometimes embarrassment is only felt in certain situations – clothes shops, for example, or meeting new people. This is often an acquired behaviour pattern from observing a parent being frequently embarrassed in a similar, though not necessarily identical, situation. The idea that this situation *should* cause embarrassment has been absorbed along with a behaviour pattern that the subconscious believes is appropriate. Again, an imprint at work.

Embarrassment is always linked to the fear of what others think or might think. Very few people become embarrassed when they are alone, but if they do, then it is nothing more than the fear of what people might think *if they knew* about whatever it is that feels embarrassing.

To help deal with it, two things are necessary. The first is a conscious recognition that these feelings are based on ideas and concepts taken on board while you were a child and are therefore no longer valid in your adult life. Second, visualisation exercises (as described in Chapter Seven) in which you see yourself remaining calm and confident in situations which you currently believe to be difficult, can be enormously helpful. A rapid-result method is to create a VMI of the archetype that is appropriate for the situation, hold it for a few moments whilst recognising how the associated attributes will be of help, then go on to the visualisation exercise itself (using an image of you, of course, *not* the archetype). Always remember that nobody knows that you feel embarrassed unless you show them!

The use of self-hypnosis will greatly improve effectiveness here, though the relaxation routine will also be quite efficient.

Fear of what others think

The fear of what others might think is strongest in the Settler and is linked to anxieties about being alone or friendless or some other way isolated from your fellow beings. *Fear of being laughed at* is the same thing, because if others are laughing at you or your ideas, then they are giving you a powerful message that you are in some way inferior, *in their opinion*. Their response to your ideas has isolated you. But there is no reason to suppose that they are right and you are wrong. Einstein was laughed at, and so was Copernicus when he stated that the Earth was round. And it was George Bernard Shaw who said, "The majority are always wrong."

Everybody suffers this particular anxiety to an extent. It can almost be considered an ancestral memory in itself, because in prehistoric times, being in accord with the rest of the tribe was essential for survival. Even the chiefs – Warrior types, mostly – would have had to rely on the support of their people if they were to continue in power. It begins to become a problem only when an individual starts to believe that his or her every action must conform to the ideas of the majority. It is based on an erroneous belief, like the overall confidence problem itself, where the individual has made up his or her own ideas about what that majority opinion would be.

In fact, the subconscious processes have little to do with other people, being centred more on the difference between what this person believes she or he should do and what she or he really *wants* to do... it is another conflict between imprint and instinct.

The 'standard' reply that a psychologist might give to someone who expressed this particular anxiety is:

What other people think, or do not think, is absolutely nothing whatsoever to do with you.

Other people's opinions about anybody or anything are based on their experiences, their judgement, and the attitudes of others towards *them*. Their thoughts are private, their own, and even if they express those thoughts, it tells you more about them than it does about you. Of course it is quite possible that you will sometimes be judged unfairly from time to time, but that is an error on the other person's part, not yours; you can allow them to make that mistake, because it does not actually make any difference to the truth, to how you really are. It is worth remembering, too, that what you fear others may think about you is quite frequently what *you* tend to think about others.

You can guarantee that for any action you take, some people would agree with it, others would disagree with it, and by far the vast majority would not give a fig. Whatever their reaction, it is irrelevant, because your decision has been made as a result of *your* life experience, *your* attitudes, etc. It may not be *exactly* what you wanted to do, it may be a compromise, but it is still your own course of action.

Fear of change

True fear of change is predominantly, though not exclusively, the domain of the Warrior. As far as this group is concerned, any change is uncharted territory where unknown perils might lurk at every turn. This feeling is linked to the ancestral memories of the Warrior tribes who needed to know as much as they could about their surroundings if they were to have the best chance of surviving the next battle, the next confrontation. In addition, of course, territorial instincts militate against leaving an area unguarded. If you are in this group and some sort of change is impossible to avoid, then deal with it via your Nomad archetype, to anticipate the exciting new opportunities that are going to present themselves. If this is difficult for any reason, then use the

Settler archetype to develop the recognition that you can easily adapt to your new circumstances. Either course will be easier if you also focus clearly on your forthright and goal-oriented Warrior attributes.

It is the negative Nomads who have the most trouble with change, even though they adore it; they never quite see anything through to completion, and are inclined to shirk their responsibilities and attempt to move on to pastures new whenever they find a problem in life. If you fall into this group, work on confidence issues generally, and develop your Settler archetype.

The Settler is usually not frightened by change, but can suffer sadness at leaving their existing established environment. If this is you and change is essential, then you will soon adapt to it, and deep inside, you are aware of this. To make the transition easier, access the bold and forthright attributes associated with your Warrior archetype.

Fear of looking stupid

Most people worry about this, but when the fear becomes strong enough to prevent you from doing things, then you need to sort it out. Most commonly with this syndrome, the actual fear is of making a silly mistake of some sort that you believe others would not make, and being seen to make it.

A mistake is something you would not have done had you known what the outcome of an event or course of action was going to be. But not knowing what the outcome was going to be is not stupid. It may be the result of being uninformed, inexperienced, unenlightened, untrained or, at the very worst, nothing more than something that has not been thought through accurately. But mistakes are never silly; they are just mistakes, an essential part of the learning process. Nobody ever became successful without making a mistake or three.

The best way to overcome the fear of making mistakes (and more often than not it is an acquired habit of thought) is to do things anyway and learn the most important lesson of all – most of the time everything is all right even if you do make a mistake, and on the odd occasion when it is not, the mistake is soon forgotten. And you have another lesson tucked away, leading you further towards success. You absolutely *have* to make mistakes in order to learn, and if one of those mistakes should happen to give someone a temporary smile along the way, just smile with them and be pleased you have lightened their day. Accessing your tolerant and forgiving Settler archetype can help here.

Low self-esteem/self-dislike

This is very common in young people, especially during their late teen years and early twenties. It will often dissipate with the growing realisation that they are no better and no worse than the average person; that they are good at some things and not others; that they can cope with some situations, yet find other situations almost unbearably uncomfortable. Usually, there is a realisation that it is all right to say "I'm not very good at this," or "That makes me feel uncomfortable." They soon come to recognise that nobody thinks any the less of them for it, and they can relax and consider themselves worthwhile people.

But when it is especially severe, maybe carrying on into mature adulthood or creating symptoms like compulsive self-mutilation (which can include tattooing and body-piercing) or other forms of self-destructive behaviour, then there is something more at the root of it. Occasionally, this is a memory of a past deed that leads the individual to believe that they are simply a 'bad person'. But think about this sentence.

"I am unworthy of this, because I did that."

Notice those mixed tenses... I *am* unworthy... I *did* that. It makes the meaning of the sentence invalid. No matter what you have done in the past, no matter how bad the deed or how many times you did those things, it is never too late to create change. Whatever you *were*, you do not have to continue to be; whatever you *did*, you do not have to continue to do. If you want to change, *truly* want to change, then you can, and if you did not have the urge to change, then you would not be considering yourself an unworthy person.

135

The fact that you feel guilt about that past deed proves that you care. The only people who should feel guilt are the ones who never do – the ones who don't care.

Quite often, self-dislike is linked to incongruence in thought processes. Thinking or rehearsing in Warrior mode whilst behaving in Settler mode, for example, can easily lead to a belief that you are weak or ineffective, because usually, in this sort of situation, your Warrior instincts are being denied. Thinking in Settler mode and behaving in Nomad mode could easily lead to feelings that you were sometimes irresponsible.

Remember, the mode in which you automatically think is likely to be the 'real' you, whereas the mode in which you behave is probably the result of imprinted behaviour. The frequent creation of a VMI of your own archetype, and recognising the attributes that you truly possess, will go a long way towards solving this problem.

Poor body image

The person with a poor body image is usually obsessed with the appearance of one particular part of their body – and it can be any part at all. It can be the shape of their nose, the thickness or thinness of their lips, the size of their feet or hands, the texture of their hair (too thick, too thin, wild, frizzy, etc.), an excess of freckles, spots, large pores... the list could go on and cover every square inch, and just about every visible feature of the entire body. It is more prevalent amongst young females, but older people and males can suffer it, too. The clinical name is *body dysmorphic disorder.*

There will often be a tendency to stare at strangers to make comparisons, as well as problems like the excessive use of cosmetics (as a sort of protective mask), extensive plastic surgery, anorexia, bulimia, and other manifestations of chronic anxiety. It does not matter how many times family and friends give reassurance, nor how many times the sufferer is told things like, "Even if that *were* true, nobody would notice..." It makes no difference. The sufferer sees what the sufferer believes is there. In fact, the sufferer sees what the sufferer *knows* is there and he or she *knows* that everybody is just trying to make them feel better about something that cannot be changed.

There is no logic in this process, though, because deep inside you, you become angry or irritated when people *cannot* see what you can see. Just think about that. *You actually tend to become angry when people cannot see what you perceive to be an unattractive part of you.* It is not unusual to feel that this physical problem is all that stops you from being attractive. Well, if that is so, *you are becoming angry when people think you are attractive*, since they cannot see the one flaw. It can sometimes feel as though you are being humoured, patronised, or that others might be making fun of you. But why would they?

To deal with this problem, it is necessary to come to terms with two important facts:

1.   The flaw that you can see so clearly is probably just one of the many normal variations that can occur in the human body, the differences make us each unique. Try this experiment: think about someone that you have compared yourself unfavourably with (in bad cases, this can be almost everybody), preferably someone that you do not know particularly well. Chances are, you have perceived them as having better hair/skin/eyes/nose/shape, or whatever feature you are focused on. But what about the rest of their body – what do you think of that? You most likely had not thought about it one way or the other until this moment. Nothing stood out. So it is fair to assume that nothing about you stood out to them.

2.   The syndrome, except in those very rare cases where everybody agrees that there is a noticeable problem, is an expression of something much deeper inside yourself. It is really another version of the 'Low self-esteem/self-dislike' problem discussed above.

To get to the root of the problem is beyond the scope of this book, because it needs the skills of a trained professional therapist, but it is certainly possible to use a bit of self-help to improve matters. If the anxiety is only slight, you may even be able to eliminate it completely. On a frequent, regular basis, try creating a VMI of your 'own' archetype, and practise visualisation exercises, where you see a VMI of yourself as looking exactly the way you actually *want* to look. Do not question it, just do it! Use as many senses as you can, and never doubt that the mind can and does create actual bodily change. You will definitely need to use self-hypnosis for this problem.

The Guilt Complex

The guilt complex accounts for a great many emotional difficulties. In fact, it is the biggest single cause of confidence problems and negative thought processes, often by generating feelings of not deserving to be successful and being in some way different to the rest of the human race. There is usually no real awareness that guilt feelings actually exist at all, in fact if guilt is mentioned, there will usually be a total denial of it. It has many symptoms, among them a tendency to wring the hands frequently (making hand-washing movements), overjustification of mistakes or errors, excessive reaction to criticism, intolerance of even the gentlest teasing and either great difficulty in admitting being wrong or a tendency to believe that anything, anywhere, that goes wrong, must be in some way their fault. This last can reach amazing proportions, where an individual may even believe that the outbreak of war somewhere is because of him or her! It is most prevalent in the Warrior personality.

The guilt complex can be alleviated, if not always completely eliminated, but that is not within the scope of this book. It is best dealt with by therapy of some sort. But recognising that it is there can help to minimise its effects, by encouraging an individual to think twice about reactions which may be attributable to it.

The foundations of the guilt complex, like the foundations of most of our psychological problems, are formed during the early years of childhood. The subconscious feelings of guilt are usually unwarranted, often associated to an event which was actually quite minor, though it was made to seem important to the child. Even where the event was fairly significant, it is still 'overblown'. There is usually no conscious memory of the originating event, and never ever any memory of the guilty associations being formed; if there were, there would be no residual guilt feelings present in later life. Problems in later life result from the subconscious attempting to discharge guilt (the single most uncomfortable emotion for the human psyche to handle) at every available opportunity – any time anything goes wrong – though there may be conscious denial, which gives rise to intolerance and difficulty in admitting being wrong, as well as other symptoms.

Frequently, a guilt complex has its origin in some childish escapade, something as simple as stealing some small item – then being terrified of being found out. Eventually the conscious memory fades but the anxiety reaction remains, flaring up every time anything goes wrong.

It can originate with sexual events: abuse or inappropriate contacts at a very young age. The way the complex forms in these cases is too complicated to go into here; suffice to say that the blame obviously lies with the perpetrator and not the victim, though the victim may well feel differently about that. By far the most common cause of the guilt complex, though – so common that almost everybody, in the Western world at least, suffers it to a degree – is masturbation anxiety. Every child masturbates. Almost every parent tells almost every child not to. And if a parent does not, then someone else probably will, usually managing to convey enough disgust or distaste to convince the child that they are in some way 'dirty'. And the odd thing is that most of the adults who are expressing distaste at what the child is doing still do it themselves (which is why they are expressing distaste – they cannot stand the reminder that they themselves are 'dirty').

As a matter of interest, the safest way to stop your own children from being embarrassing in front of friends, neighbours, relatives, etc., is to make light of it and casually say something like, "Don't do that in front of people... it's not nice in front of people." This, of course, carries the implication that it is perfectly all right to do it when they are on their own.

And of course, it IS perfectly all right for them to do it when they are on their own – whenever they like. If you have a problem with this, if you would like to stop your child from masturbating altogether, then it is you who has the problem, and you should seek help. Likewise, if you ever find yourself vigorously denying that you ever do it, even though you do, then you have a guilt/masturbation complex. And if you *Genuinely* never do it then the problem is even more profound, unless you have a sex drive of zero – and even that is a possible indicator of psychological conflict.

Whilst perhaps not being a subject for polite conversation, masturbation is a totally normal and healthy sphere of sexual activity in the human species, for both men and women. Our race is successful because we have a non-stop sex drive, not just something that occurs when the female is in season, as in other species. Our sex drive is present all the time and clamours to be satisfied even when there is no opportunity for normal sexual intercourse. Stifling that urge for sexual activity tends to create anxiety states or depression. Stifled for long enough, the urge goes away, but the anxiety or depression (or 'bad nerves') stays. And if you are female and believe that the foregoing is addressed only to the male readers... sorry, it means *you* as well.

Dealing with the guilt complex by self-help methods is not easy, but if you cannot stand being wrong, then remind yourself that being wrong is essential sometimes, that no successful person ever became successful without making mistakes. For most other symptoms, work on general confidence and self-respect, combining the VMI of your 'own' archetype with visualisation.

The Inferiority Complex

Many people claim to have an inferiority complex, but it is actually quite rare. Most of the time, the real problem is simple negativity and learned behaviour patterns, or a willingness to accept the presence of inferiority feelings as an excuse to fail. The person with a true inferiority complex honestly believes that they are simply not up to standard in *any* sphere of activity. There is an expectation that every other living soul knows more, is cleverer, more worthwhile, has more money, a better job, nicer partner, better clothes, nicer hair, better bone structure...

The good news is – it responds particularly well to self-help in the form of the frequent creation of a VMI of not just your own archetype, but of the other two as well, actually *feeling* their positive attributes and recognising that these are actually your own attributes, part of your own personality.

The very fact that you are reading this book is a sure indication that your mind will respond to this type of visualisation work; your inferiority complex is not as deep-rooted as you might have thought, or you would never have picked this book up in the first place; it would have felt like an utter and complete waste of time to even think of achieving anything worthwhile for yourself.

Secrets

Sometimes the subconscious will make determined efforts to resist any sort of change, even though the conscious mind yearns for it. This can often be the case where business, career, or material wealth is concerned. The problem is that the subconscious is infinitely more powerful than any conscious process can ever be, which allows it to undermine your efforts. There are two reasons why this might occur.

1. *The Hidden Agenda*

This is simply a 'secret' reason in your subconscious for not succeeding at what you set out to achieve. For example, if you have somehow absorbed, and truly believe, the idea that confident people are unpleasantly 'pushy' or 'not nice', then you may develop a conflict between being confident and gaining the approval of others. The hidden agenda here is to continue to be liked (or maybe not to be disliked, which is slightly different) and is common among predominantly Settler individuals. This process might be totally hidden from you until you make the conscious connection, when it becomes crystal clear – and the problem then ceases to exist. The hidden agenda is an artificial belief that has usually been passed on by parents or others who may have felt inadequate and have needed to find a 'sop' for their own ego.

Other hidden agenda 'seeds' are:

People who spend money on themselves are selfish or 'tacky'.
This conflict will inhibit one of the major drives for financial security, since it will inhibit you from enjoying the fruits of your labours.

Successful people have no real friends. Settlers are particularly affected by this one.

Rich people cannot go to Heaven or **rich people are immoral.**
Again, this can inhibit you from finding financial success.

Positive people are bombastic and disliked. Encouraged by those who seek to find an advantage in negativity, rather than face change, this one can severely interfere with self-help programmes.

Confident people are show-offs and nobody loves a show-off.
Another weak and self-interested justification for negativity. It can actually begin to create self-consciousness about anything that builds confidence!

Honest people do not succeed. This one carries the implication that if you are successful, then others will believe you to be dishonest.

Attractive people are shallow or empty-headed. This is another self-interested proclamation with absolutely no basis in fact. It can lead to determined attempts to seem unattractive. In fact, it has been shown many times that attractive people are often *more* successful than their plainer fellows.

There are many others; search your mind carefully to see what you really think or feel about what you are seeking to achieve. Imagine that you already have it, creating a 'video film' VMI of the way your life would be then, preferably using self-hypnosis. If you feel easy and relaxed all the way through the VMI, fine; but if there is the tiniest feeling that something uncomfortable is 'niggling' away inside you, keep working at it until you find out what it is. The chances are it will be an idea that is no more valid than those listed above.

2. *The Secondary Gain*

This is similar to the hidden agenda, though there is a subtle difference. The hidden agenda is usually concerned with maintaining an existing situation, whereas the secondary gain, far more prevalent in Warrior personalities than either of the other two, is an interest in gaining what is perceived to be a benefit. The secondary gain for maintaining an illness, for example, is more time away from work, school or other responsibilities. It can be either a conscious or subconscious process.

Most secondary gain behaviours have been learned during childhood, when they brought pleasure in the form of being comforted, receiving attention or avoiding punishment, humiliation, pain or other negative experiences. The symptoms could include perpetual nightmares or bad dreams, clumsiness, illness (often inexplicable and difficult to diagnose), stealing, bullying, bedwetting, outrageous behaviour, destructiveness, cruelty to animals or other children, and so on. It can often seem crazy; a child seeking attention may well commit an act guaranteed to result in severe punishment, even violence in some situations. This begins to make more sense when you realise that, as children, the survival reflex insists that it is important that adult members of the tribe know that we are there – whatever it takes.

If you had any of these behaviour patterns as a child, or others like them, then the chances are: (1) you are predominantly Warrior, and (2) you still have a tendency to operate a secondary gain situation at times. If this is the case, you need to ensure that it does not interfere with whatever it is you are seeking; by far the most destructive situation is that of seeking sympathy by having your plans go awry. It is the 'Poor little devil – it's all gone wrong again' syndrome.

If you tend to feel a strange sensation of relief when something goes wrong with a plan or idea and you no longer have to strive, a hidden agenda is likely to be present. If, however, your reaction is a vague feeling of triumph or satisfaction, or you can hardly wait to tell others of your most recent hardship, the secondary gain principle is likely to be at work.

To sort this one out, use self-hypnosis to create a VMI... of failure! Create a VMI of your latest idea or project going completely and irretrievably wrong and isolate in your mind what it is that you hope or expect to find from others by way of compensation. You will need to search your mind thoroughly and be totally honest with yourself. When you have discovered the truth, the problem will evaporate. When you have finished this exercise, even if it was not conclusive, it is very important that you create another VMI of the same situation, idea or project resulting in resounding success.

You have everything you need now to improve your personal effectiveness and the way you feel about yourself, and help your life to run more smoothly and in the direction you want it to. In the next chapter, we are going to examine how you can use these same skills in another very important way – to deal easily and effectively with stress.

Chapter Eleven
The Subconscious Computer and Stress

Every individual possesses a biological computer system which is infinitely more sophisticated and efficient than any electronic device ever built. Every individual also suffers stress from time to time. Though you may not know it, your biological computer system can deal with all forms of stress far more effectively than any form of medication ever could. Because of this, it can help you to be healthier, delay the ageing process, and lead to a longer, more active and more enjoyable life.

Man-made computers (the first of which was designed by the English mathematician and inventor Charles Babbage as long ago as 1833) are simple devices compared to the fantastic bio-machine that evolution has given us as a birthright. It is truly amazing: it monitors numerous 'housekeeping' tasks like heart rate, blood pressure, temperature, and other automatic functions via what is known as the *autonomic nervous system*; it performs and monitors a whole host of other semi-automatic functions like breathing, walking, running, bladder and bowel control and so on; it then deals with a whole range of activities too numerous to even begin to list – all the 'voluntary' actions that we perform on a daily basis. In addition to all of that, this powerful subconscious computer has a database of every skill you ever learned, an awareness of every strength and weakness, as well as having access to that most powerful of instincts, your ancestral memory traces.

It also has a colossal memory, storing away everything that was ever important to you, so that it can be recalled, used for comparisons and testing outcomes, or to find resources. And it can work quite happily without you making any real conscious effort at all – if you let it.

Winning Battles

There is nothing new about this concept; successful men through-out history have used it, even though they may not have been completely aware of it. They have used it to win battles, compose music, write novels, invent machinery, and to succeed in virtually all fields of human endeavour. Individuals such as Einstein used it, and the Greek philosopher Socrates wrote about it in about 400 BC, calling its effects "Inspiration, such as you find in seers and prophets who deliver all the sublime messages without knowing in the least what they mean". One of the most prolific users of it was the author Henry Miller, who once said of one of his works "I didn't have to think up so much as a comma or a semicolon; it was all given, straight from the celestial recording room. Weary, I would beg for a break, an intermission, time enough, let's say, to go to the toilet or take a breath of fresh air on the balcony. Nothing doing!"

Well, maybe you are not an Einstein or a philosopher; perhaps you have no ambition to write novels like Henry Miller. But you *do* have that same invaluable facet of mind and brain that inspired them to greatness – the ability to allow your own mental process-es to find the answers you need.

If you doubt this, the consider the following: you are searching in your mind for the name of, say, a film actor. It is an oddity that the harder you try, the less likely you are to succeed. (This is not a new idea, either. The psychotherapist Émile Coué, 1857–1926, wrote about the 'law of reverse effort' describing just that effect.) Eventually, you give up, saying that you will think of it later – and so you do, when you are no longer trying; the elusive name is just suddenly there in your thoughts. Or maybe you have an impor-tant problem to solve but in spite of all your best efforts, you just don't seem to be able to come up with any workable answers. So you decide to 'sleep on it', and the next morning you find yourself just somehow *knowing* how to tackle the situation.

In both those cases and many others like them, that subconscious part of your mind did not cease in its search for the answer, even though you had consciously given up. Later, it placed the answer into your conscious thought processes. And that was without you knowing how to actually use this facility consciously, or to the best advantage.Now you are going to learn how to use it consciously.

When you find out just how easy it is, it is quite likely that you will find yourself thinking along the lines of: "Hmm, I can't see this doing anything – it's too easy." If you do, dismiss the thought instantly, just as any successful person dismisses negative thoughts about absolutely anything that might lead to a sought-after goal. If you believe it will not work, then it will not – it is as simple as that, because that belief, especially if it is coupled with a statement of doubt like the one above, represents a negative programme to the very part of your mind that you want to help you.

Using it *is* astonishingly easy, but that does not mean that it is not effective.

Programming

Programming your subconscious computer is easy. The most important step is the first one, and it is sometimes only necessary to carry out this first task for the answer to be available immediately. All you have to do is write down your problem. It is very important that you actually *write it down*, rather than just 'think it through', because writing it down is the most effective way to clarify and crystallise your thoughts.

Be as concise as possible, but make sure that you include all the necessary details. If possible, it should be phrased as an either/or situation, or a question with a yes or no answer. It is usually quite easy to narrow a problem down this way and, indeed, it is part of the exercise.

Here's an example:

Let's assume that you have been offered promotion at work, but this involves moving a hundred or so miles away. The money will be better, but the housing in the area is dearer, and you have a circle of friends you would be reluctant to leave behind. In addition, you will have a longer journey to work, and you don't much like commuting. But you have been feeling restless of late, and if you turn this promotion down, you may not be offered another one for some considerable time. To cap it all, your partner is not too keen on the idea of moving but at the same time finds the idea of a better lifestyle attractive. He or she insists on leaving it up to you and promises to go along with whatever you decide, but a small voice inside you says that they are only saying that to be supportive of you and your career.

It seems complicated, and your conscious mind may reel at the thought of trying to sort out what is best, but this sort of decision-making is just the sort of thing your subconscious computer thrives on. In fact, this is not a complicated question at all; it is the simplest of all situations, requiring only a 'yes/no' response to the question, 'Shall I take this promotion?' Your subconscious computer can easily assess all the other side issues once you have completed the preparation. Writing it down will help you recognise that.

Frequently, the very act of writing the problem down will enable you to see it differently, to know which of the two choices you should make. That's the subconscious responding in the way it knows best – spontaneously. But if an answer doesn't present itself immediately, you just have to continue the exercise. Having written down the basic question, divide your piece of paper into two halves; in one half, write down all the positive aspects of making the move – more money, nicer house, better lifestyle, better position in the company, better security, etc. In the other half, put all the negative aspects – moving away from friends, more travelling, your partner not totally happy, etc. Make it as complete as possible, then try, really try, to answer the question consciously. When you are sure that you simply *cannot* find an answer you are certain of and happy about, it's time to turn the whole thing over to your subconscious computer to work on.

First create a VMI of the archetype that has the resources needed to solve the problem – if you are not sure, then use your major archetype. Hold both the problem and the VMI in your mind for a few moments, then just say to yourself that you are going to leave it to your subconscious computer to sort out. With particularly difficult situations, you can use the same procedure with the assistance of self-hypnosis or the concentration enhancer.

Now all you have to do is completely forget that the problem even exists. Just ignore it, because any further attempts at conscious solutions are going to seriously hamper the process. The subconscious would have to keep on re-evaluating what you were doing, in case there was new information available, when all you would be doing is covering the same ground and starting the search process from scratch over and again.

Timing

Timing is important. If you have a limited time to make the decision, whether it's two months or two days, then give your mind that much time, telling your subconscious computer that you need the answer by a specific time. Saying it aloud is best, but a definite and very positive thought will do. Just thinking or saying "I will have the answer to this problem in [state time]" is sufficient. Note that the statement is that you *will* have the answer; never doubt this, since that would indicate that you were searching *not* to find an answer.

When the specified time arrives, you will know the answer. You will not hear a voice or see a sign or an omen, or anything as dramatic as that. You will simply have a *feeling* of what is the right thing to do. Trust it and act upon it, because this is a communication from your deepest instinctive self, the part of you that knows everything about you and is more than able to work out what is best for you. Never doubt it, or the process will work less efficiently next time. Many people have learned, to their cost, the folly of ignoring these instinctive thought processes.

More Complex Issues

That apparently complicated problem about the career change was actually the simplest type of all: the basic question was whether to take the promotion or not; there were no other options. Had there been a possibility of taking a new job in the same area instead, then that would have made it an either/or situation; had there been three other companies clamouring for your services, then that would have been decidedly more complicated. But your subconscious would still find the answer by exactly the same method. Write down the question, the pros and cons of each situation, try to solve it, then hand it over to the subconscious with a mental instruction as to when you need a decision – and always allow as much time as there actually is. 'Hustling' will never work and may actually produce inaccurate responses.

With complex 'multiple-choice' problems, you may have to find your answer in stages, perhaps first posing the question: "Should I work for firm A or firm B?", then setting the 'winner' of that against the next one, and so on until you are left with the final, two-choice question. Or you could possibly bypass this by concentrating on whether to stay at the same company or move, then continuing as necessary.

Once you have specified your options and all the associated issues, and written everything down in as concise and clear a manner as possible, it is *inevitable* that your subconscious will provide you with the right answer. And each time you use your subconscious in this way, it becomes more efficient and more responsive, until the whole process becomes almost automatic. You may find that some answers present themselves even without your writing anything down.

Successful people do not try to solve every problem as soon as they see it – they do not have to, because they know that their subconscious will give them the solution when they need it. And because they know it, it always does, which is one of the reasons why they always seem to know just what to do and just how to do it.

The Quick Answer

From time to time, you will find yourself with a problem that needs an answer very quickly, maybe within an hour or two. You can still use your subconscious to help you. Prepare as before, being as complete as time allows. Then use self-hypnosis or the concentration enhancer, and when you are ready, create the appropriate VMI and hold both it and the problem in your mind, as before. This time, though, after a few moments, ask your subconscious for a solution *now*, without bringing logical thought to bear (you have already tried that); you will 'feel' the right choice to make within a very short space of time, possibly even instantaneously. Because there is a genuine *need* for a rapid answer, the subconscious will do its job as efficiently as ever.

When an instant decision has to be made, there is obviously little time for preparation. In this sort of situation, simply remember that your subconscious computer is always there, always working, and ask it mentally for assistance, making quite certain to *trust the answer*. You can use a simple 'thought instruction' along the lines of: "Come on, brain, give me some help with this." Because you know that that short phrase is an instruction to the subconscious, it will act as one.

This is probably a good time to repeat something that is written in the Preface of this book:

You should not dismiss any part of what you read in this book without first trying it – and genuinely suspending scepticism, cynicism, or any feeling of 'knowing' it could not work for you while you do so. Those feelings are a part of your problem, a part of why you are not yet where you want to be.

To attempt or wish to prove this book to be wrong will do no harm to the author, but you would be throwing away a vital opportunity. You should actively *want* the concept to work every bit as well for you as it does for others. So if you find a part of yourself wanting, instead, to be able to say to people, "See? I even tried this positive thinking nonsense and it still went all wrong!" then you need to remember that you may get sympathy that way – but you will never, *ever* find much else. The choice is yours.

Defining Goals

Although this chapter is mainly about decision-making and stress, it is worth realising that you can use your subconscious computer to help you define goals – to help you work out, for example, what career or job you should aim for.

For Settlers and Nomads:

First, create a VMI of your major archetype and hold it for a moment or two, then create a further VMI in action format this time, of you as you are, looking exactly as you would like to. Now use either self-hypnosis or the concentration enhancing routine, and when you are just sitting or lying quietly, let your mind wander around everything you like in life, everything that you enjoy, everything that interests you. It is not necessary to try to make sense of it, nor should you leave things out because they do not seem right for some reason. Include everything, even sexual activity! It is not necessary to work hard; it's sufficient to just allow these pleasant thoughts to drift through your mind, telling yourself after a while that you will soon know *exactly* what it is that you want from life.

For Warriors:

Use a similar method to that already described for decision-making. Write down all the available information – skills, attributes, limitations, personality group, etc. – and first try to make conscious sense of it. Be sure to set a realistic time limit. If you are not planning to do anything about your goal for six months or so, then give it six months. If the situation is more pressing, then set a shorter time, but always give the subconscious computer as much time as there actually is. Sometimes, an 'open-ended' arrangement will work well; 'as soon as possible' or 'in due course' can both work. In general, though, it is a good idea to be as specific as possible; the subconscious has difficulty in interpreting time-scales, so it is always best not to complicate the issue unduly.

Whichever method you use, it will not be very long before you begin to experience results. You will start to find yourself having ideas and creative thoughts, sudden inspirations, vivid dreams, sudden 'knowledge' about things, hunches, and other manifestations of the sort of mental activity that every successful person has. Look for them, think about them, react to them, even act upon them. The only thing you should never do is ignore them, because then the process will slow down and maybe even stop altogether. If nothing else, just write them down. To give the process a boost, do the procedure several times, but be sure to state the same time required for the answer.

Handling Stress

The subconscious computer is an excellent tool for effective and efficient stress management. Stress is now recognised as a serious problem – most medical authorities agree that as much as 90 percent of all illness may be stress-related. Two classic examples of this are stomach ulcers and migraine: although both of these conditions may have physical causes as well, they are at least partly caused by the effects on the body of psychological stress. Some research even suggests that many cancers are more prevalent in individuals who suffer high levels of continued stress, and there is no doubt that heart and other circulatory illnesses are stress-related.

It's not surprising, then, that most doctors would agree that lowering your stress level is likely to promote a longer, healthier, and more active life. And it will certainly make you *feel* better and give you a more positive mental attitude – which *definitely* delays the ageing process.

Stress is another name for 'excitation' and is therefore not related just to bad things happening in your life, but to the exciting things, too; good events do not offset bad events – they actually add to the stress level. And stress tends to make its worst effects felt not immediately, but some time over the next two years or so – yet another good reason for effective stress management.

Stress is often personality-specific. While there are many obvious events in life – such as bereavement, redundancy and financial difficulties – that will cause *everybody* stress to one degree or another, it is fair to say that each group has their own symptomatic response to stress and each group finds certain situations more stressful than either of the other two groups would. Here is a guide to the worst situations for each group, and the symptoms that are most likely to be experienced. Shortly we will have a look at personality-related strategies to relieve those symptoms.

Warrior:

Warriors are most affected by any situation in which they are subject to some form of control or attempted control, continual criticism, or major change of any sort. Good events might include sudden career success or 'escaping' from an unsatisfactory relationship.

Symptoms: Digestive-tract problems are a very common stress symptom for the Warrior – ulcers, intestinal or bowel problems, etc. Obsessive thought or behaviour patterns are also prevalent, as is bad temper.

Settler:

Settlers have great difficulty with 'people' issues, such as being out of favour or not liked; being convinced that they are behaving in a way most people would disapprove of; or falling out with friends or family. Good events are likely to be linked to family and home – marriages, births, personal successes, going on holiday.

Symptoms: The most common stress symptom for this group is depression or social withdrawal. They are also inclined to lapse into extreme negativity, which shows up as the 'I just can't cope with this any more' syndrome.

Nomad:

Boredom, restriction and image problems are the most difficult things for Nomads to deal with: not being allowed to do things, being 'shown up' in some way, being coerced into some mundane situation. Good events are likely to include receiving a personal accolade, acquiring status, cosmetic surgery, outstanding personal success.

Symptoms: Anything dramatic! Blindness, paralysis of part of the body, vomiting, outbreaks of rashes or skin complaints and various unspecified illnesses are common. Much of the time, these clear up amazingly quickly.

Stress Factors

The chart below is based on one developed some time ago to gauge an individual's likelihood of stress-related illness. It takes no account of personality types, though most of the events are universally affective. Consider the events listed and add up the 'stress factor' numbers alongside all those that have happened to you over the last twelve months.

1. *Death of spouse or partner* 100
2. *Divorce* 73
3. *Separation from spouse or partner* 65
4. *Going to prison or similar* 63
5. *Death of close family member* 63
6. *Major personal illness or injury* 53
7. *Getting married* 50
8. *Redundancy or being fired* 47
9. *Reconciliation with spouse or partner* 45
10. *Retirement from work* 45
11. *Major illness of family member* 44
12. *Pregnancy* 40
13. *Sexual difficulties* 39
14. *New family member arriving (birth, parent coming to stay indefinitely, adoption)* 39
15. *Major work adjustment of any sort* 38
16. *Major change in financial status (up or down)* 37
17. *Death of close friend* 36
18. *Career change* 36
19. *Major change in number of arguments with spouse or partner (many more or less)* 35
20. *Taking out a mortgage or major loan* 31
21. *Difficulty with mortgage repayments* 30
22. *Major change in work situation* 29
23. *Child leaving home* 29
24. *Trouble with in-laws* 29
25. *Outstanding personal success* 28

26. *Spouse or partner starting or leaving work*............26
27. *Starting or stopping formal education*..................26
28. *Major change in living conditions*........................ 25
29. *Change in personal routines*.................................24
30. *Trouble with the boss*.. 23
31. *Change in work conditions*................................... 20
32. *Moving house*..20
33. *Changing to a new school*...................................20
34. *Major change in leisure habits*...........................19
35. *Major change community activities*.................... 19
36. *Major change in social activities*......................... 18
37. *Taking out a small mortgage or loan*.................... 17
38. *Major change in sleeping habits*...........................16
39. *Major change in number of family meetings*......... 15
40. *Major change in eating habits*..............................15
41. *Going on holiday*...13
42. *Christmas*.. 12
43. *Minor law violations (involving fines, etc.)*...........11

According to some research, your probability of illness during the next two years or so is linked to your total score as follows:

0 – 150 No particular problems.
151 – 200 Mild crisis level; 35 percent chance of illness.
201 – 300 Moderate crisis level; 50 percent chance of illness.
301 + Major crisis level. 80 percent chance of illness.

Obviously, there are many variables, quite apart from personality group, because some individuals definitely handle stress more easily than others, some are naturally more healthy than others, and some just defy the rules! It should be obvious, too, that you should make every effort to avoid combining major stress factors in your life at any one time. You should always try to 'get over' one stressful event before you embroil yourself in another.

Now to the stress-management routines. There are two described here, the first being ideal for use on a day-to-day basis, to keep you feeling calm, relaxed and in control. Where you are suffering unusually severe stress along with anxiety, continuous worrying, sleep problems and the like, the second routine will be of more benefit. It is certainly not essential to use either routine on a daily basis, and either or both can be called on as and when needed.

Stress-management routine (1)

All three personality groups can use this routine just as it is.

Most days, you will find that your natural body rhythms will suggest a time for you to do this, a time when you may feel yourself 'slowing down' (in modern psychology, these are referred to as *ultradian rhythms,* and their healing potential is well documented). Go along with it if you can, because that is when the routine will be most effective. If work or other circumstances make that difficult or impossible, then at that time tell yourself you will do it just as soon as you can – and make sure that you do.

Find a comfortable, quiet place where you can close your eyes and relax, lying down if possible. Use the concentration enhancer for a few minutes. Then, when you feel ready to do so, see yourself vividly in your mind's eye, as if you have actually left your body and are looking at yourself steadily relaxing. Tell yourself you're now handing over control to your subconscious computer so that it can get on with its maintenance of mind and body, just as it does while you sleep. It is rather like having workmen in to do a few small repairs while you go for a walk.

Now do nothing for as long as it takes.

You will find that after a period of between 20 and 45 minutes, your eyes will just open naturally of their own accord, signalling that the restoration work is complete. You should now recover yourself to full awareness, when you will feel invigorated and relaxed, with increased enthusiasm, concentration and alertness. But don't be tempted to close your eyes again, or you *could* find the just the reverse, ending up headachy and 'muzzy'.

Stress-management routine (2)

This routine is more powerful and requires a preparation stage; although all personality groups could use any one of the three described, the results will be better if you use the one recommended for your group.

Warrior: Use the standard concentration enhancer.

Settler: The preparation routine for Method 1 of achieving self-hypnosis, found in Chapter Eight, is best for this group. You do not need the relaxation phase.

Nomad: Method 2 in Chapter Eight will work very well. You don't need the preparation routine; just settle yourself quietly and go straight to the breathing process.

When you are ready, follow with this short routine described below, which will actually produce a state of deep relaxation and well-being. If you have practiced self-hypnosis, you will notice certain similarities. Learn the routine off by heart, rather than record it, because then you can use it whenever you want to.

Imagine, as vividly as you can, that you are at the top of a beautiful, warm, softly lit staircase with ten steps to go down, all covered in a beautifully soft carpet in your favourite colour and design, with a wonderfully smooth hardwood handrail at the side. At the bottom of the staircase is a door, and behind the door is a room, your own special room, where nobody but you ever goes. In your mind, move slowly down the staircase, telling yourself that with each step you take you are more relaxed than on the stair above; feel the carpet beneath your feet and your hand gliding down the handrail as you move. Take plenty of time.

At the bottom of the staircase you find yourself in front of the door to your own special room. Take time to study it for a moment, noticing the texture and pattern of the handle, and tell yourself that this room is always here for you in your thoughts, that you can always find it just by going down that staircase of calmness and relaxation in your mind. Then open the door and move easily inside the room. It is comfortable and warm inside, softly lit, and furnished exactly as you want it to be to make it absolutely perfect.

Make it truly vivid in your mind, using as many senses as you can, because this is a room where you can make wonderful things happen for yourself, just by imagining them.

In the middle of the room is a comfortable chair, the most luxurious and comfortable chair you have ever seen, and you dawdle lazily over to it and flop yourself down, marvelling at the deep sense of tranquillity that sweeps over you as you become more relaxed than you can ever remember.

Now just empty your mind – you can do this easily in this super-relaxed state. Say the following positive suggestions to yourself several times each – in full and aloud if possible. The third one is rather lengthy, but learn it, because it is extremely powerful. Create a VMI of you looking exactly as you want to be, and hold it in your mind while you repeat the suggestions.

Things that can be changed *will* change, because I will change the things that I can change.

Things that cannot be changed will simply cease to concern me.

All the things that used to upset me will now just calm and relax me, and the more they previously upset me, the more they will now simply calm and relax me.

When you have finished the suggestions – and your mind will usually know when that is – turn yourself over to the subconscious computer as in Method 1, except that you will need to take yourself out of the relaxed state when you are ready to leave it.

The above is a powerful 'stress-busting' routine that you can use as often as you like. You will find that your imaginary room becomes steadily more complete and more relaxing, and that you can eventually just go directly to it without using the preparation, relaxation and stairs first.

This chapter has shown you how to deal effectively with the vast majority of stress situations, even when the stress is quite severe. In Appendix 2, at the back of the book, there is an in-depth look at some specific psychological difficulties, including panic attacks, habits and shyness.

Chapter Twelve
Hanging It All Together

The main purpose of this final chapter is to reflect on all you have discovered about yourself and others, the uses you can make of that knowledge, and a little more about change and how to create it and sustain it. There is also an idea or two to help you look at problems from a different angle.

If you have already conducted the self-discovery tests and worked at the self-therapy routines throughout the book, then you are probably becoming quite adept at using the VMI and relevant archetypes to start creating the changes you need. You are almost certainly a Settler personality and quietly accepting the fact that permanent change takes a little time to achieve.

If, on the other hand, you have simply been reading through the book first, so that you can get a good idea of what it is all about before you actually do anything, then you are probably a Warrior. If you are also prone to negativity in your Warrior thought patterns, then you are in danger of putting the book on the shelf (to gather dust with the other self-help books) after you have finished reading this chapter, because Warriors seek to resist change. Of course, you will do something about it 'one of these days'... When you have more time. When the time is right. When you have got that other pressing business over and done with so that you can give it your full concentration. What you really mean is that, once again, as always, you have discovered there is a snag... you have to do something and you have to change.

There are many reasons (excuses) why an individual may decide not to pursue a plan for self-improvement. Among them are:

- It wouldn't work for me.
- It'd take too long and be too difficult.
- I don't see how this can possibly make any worthwhile difference.

- It's just the way I am – it's pointless trying to change now.
- I'm too old to change.
- I'm just not a successful person – I think I must be jinxed.
- I might end up worse off.-
- There's always a snag to this sort of thing.

All those excuses, and others like them, are nothing more than resistance to change coming from the Warrior area of your personality, whatever your major group is. As illogical as it is, it is not at all unusual for people to wish for great improvement in their life and yet to be unable to contemplate the idea of anything changing!

Nomads have a different problem; they will start out eagerly and with great enthusiasm but will lose impetus quite quickly, usually when something else grabs their attention or when results are not immediately noticeable. In fact, change *will* usually happen fairly quickly for the Nomad, just not quickly enough! Then the plan is dropped and the search for something else begins... You need to accept, though, that if you have been encouraged for the whole of your life to behave in a mode that does not quite fit your instincts, or if you learned while growing up that the way you behave is somehow not desirable, then lasting change will take longer than the time it takes to read this book.

A Helping Hand

You can use your archetypes to help you with the process of adjustment. If you are a Warrior, then what if you adopted some of the exuberance of your Nomad archetype and the adaptability of your Settler? And how fantastic the Nomads' success could be if they combined their enthusiasm and vitality with the tenacity of the Warrior and the diligence and patience of the Settler! The Settlers have it best of all, in many ways, because all they have to do is to recognise that they can adopt the Warrior's resolve and combine it with the sheer joy of being alive that is so often exhibited by the Nomad in order to find a true and lasting contentment.

Here are some specific hints for success for each group.

Warrior:

It is important for you to recognise that if you are to achieve anything worthwhile, you have a far harder task than those rough, tough ancestors of yours. They already knew what life held in store, because then, it was just a question of survival of the strongest. Once your enemy was vanquished you were home and dry until there was another challenge or challenger. Their major attributes were force and control. But now things are different. You need to tolerate and communicate, using the skills of your Settler, and you need the expressive abilities of the Nomad to impress and inspire. In this way, you can become truly successful, especially in the material sense.

Warriors quite often have difficulty in accepting or admitting that their instinctive way of dealing with a problem is not necessarily the best way. To overcome this failing, remember that the most successful of your ancestors were those with the greatest resources, and that you have potentially far greater resources than they ever did – the resources of the other two 'tribes', in fact, as well as your own. Always develop the archetypes associated with your second and third groups as fully as you possibly can, *and use them where necessary*; it may be that you will have to work hard at the least prominent, but the effort will be repaid. Treat them as your 'secret weapons' that you can bring to bear whenever you want to, so that neither the most impressive Nomad nor the most versatile Settler will ever be able to 'get the better' of you – because you will always be able to use your Warrior's speed of thought to out manoeuvre the Settler and outshine the Nomad *on their own ground*, when their particular attributes might otherwise have won the day. In general, during any interaction with others, you would observe the mode of the individual you are talking to and act or react accordingly.

Probably the most important thing for Warriors is to admit any negative traits that you have discovered, because you will not be able to do anything about them until you do. Study the description of the negative attributes in Chapter Two and be ruthlessly honest with yourself – then seek a way to offset them. You can use affirmations, a VMI, or the Swish technique. Of course, you have to actually want change in order to achieve it, and it may be that you actually *like* the negative traits you find – a situation that is not at all unusual for the Warrior personality. In that case, if you need to 'override' your natural tendencies at any time, you should access the archetype who possesses the *opposite* attributes.

When confronted with a problem, Warriors have a tendency to see it from only one viewpoint, and to therefore seek the answer from that viewpoint; this is usually an attempt to gain some sort of control or domination over the situation. Where a solution is not immediately apparent, it is good idea to first of all analyse it. If it is multifaceted, or concerned largely with a Settler individual, then you need to access the Settler archetype; if it is concerned in some way with presentation of either yourself or something you have done or intend to do, then your Nomad archetype will probably provide the answer. Use self-hypnosis (or the concentration enhancer), then create a VMI of the relevant archetype and hold it in your mind whilst considering the problem. If a workable solution does not occur to you, then it is time to employ the subconscious computer (Chapter Eleven) to sort it out.

As far as material success is concerned, you will always do best in areas where your advanced perception, logic and practical abilities can be brought into play. These include all forms of engineering (including computer programming), building, quality control, detection, security, surveillance, legal or disciplinary matters, military, mathematics, financial matters (control, not investment), manufacturing, business management, competitive sports.

This is not to say that a Warrior cannot be successful in other fields, just that there is obviously a *greater* chance of success in those areas which rely heavily on your natural attributes.

Settler:

You probably have an easier task than either of the other two groups when it comes to finding success, especially if you feel that contentment and happiness are part of the recipe – which the vast majority of Settlers do. Warriors are usually too busy bemoaning what they have not got to ever enjoy what they have; Nomads are all right while they are able to indulge themselves or as long as they are being entertained or entertaining in some way, but they are not easily able to tolerate 'ordinariness' for very long without becoming fed up. Settlers, of course, can find joy and contentment almost wherever they are and are particularly adept at finding the silver lining without even noticing the cloud that brought it in the first place! When it comes to making the best of things, in whichever way anybody can look it, the versatile and adaptable Settlers simply have no equal.

The sad part about it all is that, in negative mode, you can too easily fail to realise just what a grand job you are doing and might spend ages labouring under the illusion that you have let yourself and others down, that you should have been more conscientious and less selfish. The famous 'all or nothing' response pretty much guarantees that if something does not work out as you think it should, then you will decide that the whole thing is a waste of time. When the Settler is in negative mode, there are no degrees of success – things are either good or bad, and if they are bad, then they are totally bad.

Settlers never have any difficulty in recognising their negative traits; quite the reverse, in fact, since they often seem all too eager to embrace them! But if this is you, be wary, because this tendency to self-denigration or self-effacement does not always do what it is designed to do. Usually, it is an attempt not to offend another in some way. There is a wish not to seem too clever, too intelligent, too financially successful, too *anything*, in case it makes somebody else feel inadequate or in case it attracts some form of denigration or admonishment. Settlers tend to take everything to heart and can easily feel great guilt if they believe they have upset somebody in any way whatsoever.

But a self-effacing approach, whereby you almost apologise for your own success or good fortune, can lead to others actively resenting what you have or achieve – which is, of course, the very situation you have set out to avoid in the first place! In addition, this approach is extremely self-limiting, because it will eventually lead to the avoidance of success, in the hope that this will allow you to be accepted more readily by your fellows. It never works. So perhaps the most useful change the Settler can make is to recognise that everybody is perfectly entitled to enjoy success that they have achieved by their own efforts, and if they achieve their success easily, then that is exactly what they deserve.

Settlers will often complicate problems unnecessarily, seeking to please not only themselves but everybody else as well. They will look at the situation in hand from every conceivable angle and eventually arrive at a great truth – you cannot please all the people all of the time! Adopt the right mode: Warrior for decisions based upon known facts when an uncompromising 'yes' or 'no' is needed, and Nomad when it comes to matters of spontaneity or image concerns. For almost anything else, your own group is the best and most versatile problem-solver. It goes without saying that you will use the VMI as effectively as it can be used, and when you simply cannot arrive at a satisfactory solution, then it is time to hand it over to the subconscious computer (Chapter 11) to look after.

Where material success or careers are concerned, the Settler excels in all areas where communication and understanding of others come into play. These include: all forms or writing and journalism (except technical), most forms of psychotherapy, nursing, teaching, philosophy, troubleshooting, industrial/work/customer relations, counselling, retail sales, welfare and social work, and almost everything to do with the caring professions. Working the land in some way is also an option.

The adaptability of the Settler ensures that success can be found in a great many fields, but it will always be enjoyed and accepted more when it is associated with occupations similar to those listed above.

Nomad:

Success, for the Nomad, is being able to have what you want the moment you want it, and having to wait for anything at all can seem almost unbearable and certainly worth a tantrum or two! Unfortunately, these subconscious drives can actually militate against any lasting success, because no sooner do you get things the way you thought you wanted them, than you decide that either (a) it was not what you wanted after all, or (b) it is time for another change! Lasting success requires stability, but stability can get uncomfortably close to being boring, which is something else the Nomad personality type abhors.

It is difficult for you to look at anybody else with a view to learning from their example; if you are honest with yourself, you will readily accept that you are inclined to be self-oriented. But learning from others is exactly what is needed if you are to eventually have the best of everything. The best thing Nomads can ever do is to recognise that their ability to enthuse and inspire others is unsurpassable. No problem there. Now imagine how incredibly impressive that attribute can be if it is linked to the admirable determination of the Warrior types and the astounding adaptability of the Settler. So, although it might stretch your patience just a touch, you, more than the other two groups, will benefit *hugely* from developing your other two archetypes.

You will probably derive the greatest benefit from the influence of the Warrior, and you could do no better than spend a little time each day just holding that VMI in your mind and sensing the associated attributes. As well as being able to impress others better than anybody else can, you are also unsurpassed as a mimic and actor, and these skills are going to be of immense use to you in assimilating something of the determination of this particular archetype. The Settler archetype will be of great use, too, and if you can do nothing more than access that adaptability and versatility when you need it, it will still pay huge dividends.

When dealing with any sort of problem, the tendency of the Nomad is to find the quickest fix possible, even if it is obvious that this will only provide a temporary solution. Sometimes, this can lead to all sorts of 'bodge' jobs performed by 'cowboys' – that term itself is perfect for the type, since the cowboy of the old West just has to be one of the greatest of Nomads in recent history. Always try to ensure that you produce your best work, even when it is something that is not going to be seen, and always seek solutions that will last longer than you think necessary. To help in this, access the Warrior and Settler archetypes (Warrior for practicality, Settler for conscientiousness) and create a VMI of the task being performed as soundly as possible. Your subconscious will provide the answer, and you should be sure to follow those instinctive thoughts if things are not to 'backfire' on you later. Most modern Nomads do not have the luxury of continually moving on from their inefficiencies.

It can be difficult for you to even recognise negative traits, never mind actually do anything about them. The most common is the 'headline but no story' attitude, the situation that can result in idle boasting about overblown or even completely non-existent achievements. To you it may feel like just a bit of fun or 'embroidery' of a tale – if you ever think about it at all; but it can easily lead to others viewing you as being an idle boaster of no consequence, an irritating individual not be trusted or taken seriously.

Outstanding material success can be found in such areas as acting, 'glitzy' presentation, direct sales, product launches, publicity work, all entrepreneurial activities, entertainment, advertising and promotion agencies, dancing and other artistic 'athletics', graphic design, fashion, modelling and just about anything to do with any form of presentation of self or others.

The Continuation of Success

Whatever success means for you, and whatever sort of success you seek, you now have everything you need to find it and maintain it. You have archetypes with attributes that allow you to deal with just about every situation you will ever encounter; you have the 'psycho-switch', the 'four-sense' test for success, the ability to use the VMI and other visualisation skills, self hypnosis, an understanding of positive thinking, positive affirmations, and more.

Accessing your archetypes is central to the type of self-therapy taught in this book, and it should become an automatic process if you do the conscious part of the work properly. If it does not, then you have not yet created them vividly enough, or you have not yet recognised the value of each. If you find one of them difficult to create in the first place, then you need to work harder at the development of that one if you are not to miss out on some of your rightful resources, your ancestral memories and instincts. Even your least dominant archetype deserves development, and the stronger you can make it the more you will be able to access the associated attributes.

You will need to access your archetypes less and less as time goes by, because the associated attributes steadily become a more permanent part of your personality; this will just happen naturally and gradually, and there is no need for you to encourage the process in any way. The day will come when you realise that there is one that you have not even thought about for some time (usually that of your major personality group), and there may even be an awareness that you can actually 'let go' of that particular imaginary individual. In general, your least dominant will remain with you the longest, and there may be a need to keep this one active indefinitely through occasional VMI work. This is especially true in the case of the Settler with the secondary Nomad and a very low Warrior score in the personality test in Chapter Two; it is also often true of the Nomad/Settler type. You will need your Warrior if you are to maintain the success this book will help you create. You will need it to help with resolve when dealing with other Warriors or with difficult situations; you will need it when you have to make awkward choices; and most of all, you will need it to keep a practical eye on all your endeavours.

What is certain is that whatever personality group you are, you should always allow yourself the advantages that come from the use of visualisation and the creation of the appropriate VMI. This is what successful people the world over do, momentarily visualising the desired outcome of a plan or concept so vividly and positively that the image needs to last for only fractions of a second. In that brief time-span the instruction to seek success is placed in the subconscious, and the goal-directed response will start in that very instant.

So there you have it – a game plan to get exactly what you want from life. It may not necessarily be astoundingly easy (though it might be!) to get from where you are to where you want to be, but, then again, it will not be that difficult either. And you can be sure that the journey will be enjoyable.

Appendix

Appendix One
Exercises to Improve Visualisation Skills

Some people believe that they simply cannot visualise anything, that their imagination will not allow them to create images of any sort in their mind; but that is just another error of the fundamental belief system. Visualisation is linked to, and used in, the process of recognition, so an individual who was totally devoid of the skill would not be able to perform even the simplest of recognition tasks. They would not know, without testing, whether a cat's fur felt more like silk or sandpaper; nor could they tell you, without looking, whether a ball is a different shape to an egg. They could not even describe a film they had seen. The film, in fact, would have made no sense to them at all, since they would not have been able to remember the actors from one scene to the next.

When you were born, before you even knew what language was, your brain was already a fully functioning organ. But precisely *because* you knew no spoken language, the only way you could think was in images, in pictures; thinking in pictures is part of the visualisation process that every human being possesses as a birthright – an ancestral skill.

So if you believe you cannot 'see' pictures in your mind's eye, it is only because you have forgotten how – not forgotten how to do it, but forgotten how to control it. If you can think of a milk bottle and know whether it is empty or full; if you can describe your place of work; if you can remember some of the details of an advert on TV; if you know what you look like when you see yourself in the mirror (if you didn't, then you'd get a surprise whenever you see yourself!) – these are all excellent examples of the visualisation process at work. But they seem so normal that they can pass unnoticed, just like breathing or swallowing.

If you still doubt that you can see things without them actually being there, what must be happening when you dream? Dreaming is nothing more than the visual centres of the brain being stimulated by the action of the mind, though to an extraordinary degree, certainly far greater than conscious visualisation will do. And to those readers who might now be saying: "Aha! But I don't dream, you see!" ask yourself (and be sure to find the answer) why you should feel so triumphant at discovering that something which could help to get you all that you want, seems to be unavailable to you. It is an established fact that *everybody* dreams, though some people do not remember their dreams.

The exercises described here will help to improve your visual imagination, to develop your mind's eye to its maximum potential. They move from easy to more difficult, so feel free to 'skip' over them until you find your level.

1. Place a familiar object on a table in front of you – a pen, a vase or an ornament of some sort. Study it and notice as much as you can about it – colour, shape, size, etc. Now move it out of your vision and try to recall as many of those details as you can. Do not rely on memorizing a mental 'list' of characteristics, because that is the very reason you are having trouble 'seeing' things in the first place – you are using your logical processes. Instead, search in your mind for an image or a 'feel' of what that object was like and recall the details by studying that mental image. You already do this whenever you describe anything to someone else. Now, can you:

    a) Imagine it in a different colour?
    b) Imagine it bigger or smaller?
    c) Imagine it standing upside down or on its side?

    If you answered 'no' to any of those questions, try again and practise until you can perform those tasks easily.

2. Look at a picture in the newspaper – it does not matter whether it is a person, a scene, an object or an advertisement, but make sure that it is black and white. Now imagine it in colour, closing your eyes if that helps. When you can do that, imagine that it is 'live' and in front of you; or, if it is a scene of some sort, imagine that you are there. You will probably find this easiest with things you are interested in and familiar with. It does not matter what you

choose; if using your imagination is easier with a picture of an attractive person, that that is as good a way as any to practise!

3. Look at any item of furniture in your house and perform the following imagery 'tricks' with it, again closing your eyes if that helps.

    a) Imagine it in several different colours in succession.
    b) Imagine what a photograph of it would look like.
    c) Imagine it floating in mid-air.
    d) Imagine the room without it.
    e) Without looking, write a description of it, then check it to see how accurate you were.

4. Without going to look first, write down a description of any room in your house other than the one you are in. Try to get the approximate size, the colours and textures of the walls, the furniture and other items. This is a difficult exercise unless you have at least average visualising ability. Almost everybody will get a few details wrong, but that does not matter, because you are still exercising the right part of your Intelligence Engine.

5. Now imagine yourself looking at a photograph or a picture. Imagine that scene, or part of it, moving. If you find this difficult, then start with a newspaper or magazine picture in front of you – it does not matter of what, as long as it would be logical for part or all of the scene to be moving in some way. A landscape scene, for instance could have moving vehicles, animals, leaves on trees, clouds, windmill sails, etc. Now for a 'toughie'. Switch on the TV and wait until there is a scene with activity going on, then imagine it going into 'freeze-frame' mode. Now make it black and white... then increase the colours to excessive vividness before returning it to normal. Close your eyes if it helps.

6. Look out of the window of any room of your house and imagine that the season has suddenly changed. Imagine the colours of any trees or foliage, what people would be

wearing, how they would be moving, what the ground would look like, what the rooftops would look like, etc., and make it as vivid as you possibly can. Now *imagine* looking out of any other window in your house and do the same mental imagery tricks with that scene. (To complete this part of the exercise successfully, you must be able to do this without going to look out of the window first.)

7.   This is one of the most difficult of visual sense imagery exercises. You need to find a fairly good-sized picture to study – it does not matter too much what it is a picture of, but it does need to be in colour, and it needs to be pleasing to your eye. Study it, looking for patterns of light and shade, shapes and angles. For instance, in a landscape, look for patterns in the trees. There may be patterns in the way that animals are standing or lying. It does not matter if you cannot, at first, see any of these patterns, because the act of searching for them is exercising your visual senses. Now try to see 'hidden' parts of the picture – the rest of the cloud that is behind a hill, or the part of the field that is behind the barn, the part of the stream obscured by rocks or animals, etc. Lastly, and most difficult, try to *feel* what the picture conveys to you by imagining that it is 'live' in front of you, or that you are there. If it is a painting, try to guess or feel what the artist was trying to tell the viewer, what feelings or atmosphere he or she was seeking to convey.

8.   Look at a chair. Now imagine yourself sitting on that chair looking:

     a)   Just the way you usually look.
     b)   Fed up or bored, waiting for something to happen.
     c)   Angry, annoyed, irritated or impatient because it hasn't happened yet.
     d)   As if you have just won £5,000,000!

Increasing Versatility

The exercises you have just completed are the most essential ones for visualisation techniques, and you should make sure that you practise them frequently until seeing images in your mind's eye is second nature to you.

There are two other very useful exercises that will increase the versatility of this creative part of your brain.

1.   Sit comfortably on a straight-backed chair, with your feet flat on the floor, and centre your vision on any object. Now keep your gaze focused on that object and investigate what else you can see *without moving your eyes*. You will probably find it somewhat difficult to 'take in' and make sense of more than one item at a time at first, and it is quite usual, as you concentrate on the edges of your vision, for whatever is in the centre to seem somehow 'out of focus'. Try the same thing with sounds, listening to the radio and the TV at the same time, for example, and trying to make sense of both, or each separately. You will find that both visual and aural skills will improve considerably with practice, proof that the right half of your brain is beginning to work efficiently.

2.   Sit or lie in a comfortable position with your eyes closed, concentrating on your breathing for a minute or two; breathe evenly and steadily until you feel yourself becoming very relaxed. Imagine that you are trying to convince somebody that you are sound asleep. Now do nothing (don't even fall asleep!). You will soon discover that you cannot actually do *nothing*, unless you have already practised meditation for a good few years, because it is difficult to get your mind to switch off. What will happen is that random thoughts will begin to present themselves to you and may even do so the moment you close your eyes, before you have even started to truly relax.

These thoughts can take literally thousands of different forms, so it is impossible to give useful examples here; in any case, it is quite unimportant. If you have done the previous exercises properly, you will find that you can easily create pictures associated with these thoughts – in fact, it is quite likely that you will not be able to *stop* those images forming, since this is a natural and inborn aspect of human brain activity. Remember, you will only be imagining what things would look like if they *were* there, so you will not see 'virtual reality' images that are sustained to the point where it is like looking at a TV screen, or real life.

If you are one of the rare people who, even after reading this far, still finds it difficult to create these images, go back to the beginning of this appendix and start again. The fact that you can identify objects – even the words on this page – proves that your visual imagery centres work perfectly well. If they didn't, you would constantly be wondering what everything is! When you look at anything, it is compared, in a fraction of a second, with every one of your stored images. If it fits any of them, you can identify what you are looking at; if it does not, then you cannot, and it is stored as a new image for further comparisons. There is even a counting device for the number of times you have accessed each image, which is how you can know that "I've only ever seen three of these before." So if you haven't yet been successful, try again. It *does* work and it *will* work. The very fact that you can understand these words proves it.

Assuming that you are now able to create images from random thought, we can now move on; think a thought you have *decided* to think and make a picture out of it. Hey presto! That is exactly the sort of visualisation technique you need to make your plans work. And if you find yourself saying at this moment, "Is that all visualisation is? Well I could always do that – I was expecting something different" – do not worry. Thousands of others have been down this route before you, and it was absolutely necessary to do it in order to know that you had got it right.

Appendix Two
Psychological Symptoms

There is no reference to specific character types in this chapter, since the problems listed can be experienced by just about anybody. If you suffer from any of the problems listed here, it is advisable to consult your GP to ensure that there is no underlying physical cause. A number of clinical conditions can create symptoms that may appear to be psychological.

In this chapter, you will find advice and help for a variety of problems that are often of psychological origin. Most of them would only truly benefit from the attention of a professional therapist, but having some understanding of them can lessen their effects.

The use of self-hypnosis will bring great improvement to almost everything listed here; the concentration enhancer is unlikely to be as effective, though it would better than nothing. Considerable space is given to the first of these psychological problems; it is one of the most common and most debilitating, and something that can be suffered by all personality groups equally.

Panic Syndrome and Panic Attacks

The full-blown panic attack has to be one of the most dramatic manifestations of the effect the subconscious can have upon the mind and body. The symptoms can include dizziness, sweating, hot flushes, fast heart rate (tachycardia), fast breathing (hyperventilation), feelings of breathlessness, legs and arms turning to jelly, trembling, clammy palms, diarrhoea, vomiting, nausea, visual disturbance, paralysis, whole-body tingling, numbness, 'creeping' sensations on the skin (especially the scalp)... and the most obvious and distressing symptom of the lot – F E A R.

Victims cannot tell anybody what they are frightened of; there is nothing rational about any of it. But anybody who thinks that sufferers should simply 'pull themselves together' has not the vaguest idea of what an attack of this sort actually *feels* like. You might just as well ask someone to be unconcerned about a herd of wild elephants charging straight at them, or about the fact that they have just fallen out of a twelfth-storey window.

It is a self-cycling phenomenon in more ways than one. After each attack, the sufferer begins to dread the next, being absolutely certain that it is going to be at least as bad as the last and probably worse. There is an almost constant searching of the psyche and body to see if there is an indication of imminence; under these circumstances, even the tiniest change that takes place somewhere in the body is instantly noticed. And that change is likely to promote the next attack – that phrase 'Be careful what you look for, in case you find it' is very important here.

Another way that the panic attack self-cycles is in blood chemistry. Fear initiates the fight-or-flight reflex, and this produces a surge of adrenalin and nor-adrenalin to help us deal with whatever is promoting the fear. (There does not actually have to be anything to be frightened of, merely a feeling of fear for this to happen.) The autonomic nervous system then causes the breathing rate to speed up – so that our body has enough oxygen to deal with the perceived threat – and when the breathing rate speeds up, the rate of oxygen exchange in the lungs increases. Now the heart has to speed up in order to keep pace with this, and the speeded-up heart rate is instantly noticed by the victim and translated as fear, which produces a surge of adrenalin...

When it comes to a battle between imagination and will-power, imagination will win every time, so it is no good repeatedly telling a sufferer (even if the sufferer is yourself) that there is nothing to be frightened of, so just calm down. The imagination is working overtime by now, producing a feeling, an overwhelming certainty, that something awful is about to happen.

Preventive measures:

Understanding is more than half the battle of dealing with this symptom and is probably the best preventive measure of all. Understanding that the whole thing is triggered by the primitive fight-or-flight reflex, which was actually designed to protect our species; understanding that no actual harm can come to you, even though it feels like it can; understanding of the self-cycling nature of the beast, so that you can actually take steps to combat what is happening; understanding that however bad it gets, it *will* pass; and understanding that the mind and body simply *cannot* sustain these feelings indefinitely – they do *have* to stop. Understanding all these things can help enormously. Get any one attack under control and you will gain confidence; this will make the next one easier to deal with, and you will then gain even more confidence... and so on.

Some people rely on medication, which can work astonishingly well in many cases, especially with some of the newer drugs that are becoming available. The snag here is that the body may become used to the drugs, so that they *may* become less effective over a period of time. There are also, of course, other problems with this type of treatment, in the form of side-effects, addiction, and so on.

Where the attacks are an 'acquired behaviour pattern', i.e. where they have been learned in some way, self-help can eventually banish them altogether. Sometimes, though, they are the result of a deeply buried memory of some anxiety or other. The actual event may have been very minor, but at the time – usually during the formative years – created a huge amount of anxiety. Where this is the case, the only truly effective method of treatment is analytical therapy, which can have the most amazingly beneficial results, transforming a sufferer's life to an apparently miraculous degree. This is how many therapists routinely treat people for this particular symptom, and the success rate is extremely high. There are also other forms or therapeutic intervention. Whatever method is used, it is possible to banish attacks *completely and forever*, whether they are an acquired behaviour pattern or the result of a deeply buried memory 'trigger'.

Dealing with an attack:

Once an attack has started, the fear tends to self-cycle rapidly, leaving the sufferer feeling totally helpless and out of control. If you ever have this feeling, remember that it is *your* body that is doing this, *your* subconscious reactions, *your* irrational fear... so it

181

is actually *you* who are controlling it. You are not controlling it in the way you want to, but that is only because you have practised panicking, rather than relaxing. But you can make changes in the way you do things.

Do not fight it:

One method that can be astonishingly effective for some people is to simply not bother trying to control it at all. Just let it run. One of the reasons that a panic attack can grow to such enormous proportions is that you fight against it; if you fight something, your subconscious believes there is something to fight, something to fear. And then, of course, the fight-or-flight reaction comes into play, starting with that surge of adrenalin.

So you could just sit down and observe your physical reactions with interest and wonder how long your subconscious is going to be able to maintain it. Do not be afraid – this is actually much easier than it sounds if you remember that no actual harm can come to you during an attack. For some people, as soon as you decide to just let it 'run its course', the whole thing subsides instantly.

Breathe easily:

Controlling your breathing is an excellent way to bring an attack under control, because it is the easiest component of the 'attack' to bring your mind to bear upon. Try this: breathe out, all the way, then hold your breath *out* for several seconds before slowly breathing in. The in-breath should be slow enough that if a feather was held in front of your nostrils, it would not move. Then exhale steadily and in a relaxed manner. Repeat the exercise, always breathing in slowly. Once the breathing is steady, the heart rate will rapidly slow down and the blood chemistry will soon correct itself.

Exercise it away:

Since part of the cause of the panic sensation is the body's preparation for physical activity such as running or fighting, you can do a lot worse than exercise for a few minutes, to 'burn off' the adrenalin and other chemicals. Some people actually feel a distinct urge to run when an attack starts. You can jog on the spot, or around the block, hop from foot to foot for a little while, or perform just about any other physical activity that would cause you to warm up and breathe harder than usual. But only attempt this method if you are at least reasonably fit.

Visualisation:

Create a VMI of absolute tranquillity – a beautiful, calm lake surrounded by tall trees with mist-covered hills in the distance; a beautiful beach on a tropical island where you can just sit and watch the ocean; floating in a small boat along a trickling stream in warm sunshine; lying on a grassy bank somewhere, listening to the sounds of nature; floating on air and just drifting, with nobody wanting anything and nobody expecting anything; staring lazily into a fish-pond on a warm summer day, watching the fish and listening to the small fountain that plays into the pond...

All these are useful images, and you can probably think of many more that may be even more relaxing for you. Make it vivid in your mind and really concentrate on it, and your panic will soon subside. Once you have created your VMI, it is there, of course, whenever you need it.

Another way of working is to use self-hypnosis at some time when you are not feeling any signs of panic. Create your VMI and tell yourself that whenever you see it in your mind's eye you will instantly feel as totally calm as you do at the moment you create it.

Go out of body: Sit or lie down, close your eyes, and imagine that you are drifting out of your body. Give yourself plenty of time;there is no need to hurry. Now, just imagine that you are drifting outside yourself, that you can actually *see* yourself... and do whatever you need to do to be steadily more relaxed. Maybe you need to slow your breathing down – see that happening and hear it, too. Perhaps your arms and legs look stiff, so relax them. You can pretend to be sound asleep – and see yourself pretending so convincingly that anybody watching you would move quietly and speak softly so as not to disturb you. When you feel calm again – usually within just a few moments – drift down into your body in your mind and open your eyes.

There are many other ways of dealing with panic attacks, but most of them are based around the methods described here. One of them, or even a combination of two or more, should prove effective for you, but remember that these are only ways of dealing with attacks, not banish them completely – though this may happen as you learn to fear attacks less.

Phobia

The phobia is the close cousin of the panic attack. Whereas the panic attack is the result of what used to be called 'free-floating anxiety', the phobic response actually triggers irrational panic reactions. If someone is outdoors when their very first panic attack starts, they may well begin to suffer from *agoraphobia* (fear of open spaces). If they are in a lift, they might develop *claustrophobia* (fear of small spaces). Many phobic responses are born this way.

The reaction is almost identical to a panic attack, except that the sufferer knows where the fear is coming from, even though they may not be able to say why. The fear may well be irrational. One individual who could not get into lifts protested that his fear was rational, because war could break out, the building he was in might get bombed, and he could be trapped. His phobia ceased when someone pointed out that the steel cage of the lift would protect him until help came.

When you think about it, a phobia is an extremely efficient way for the subconscious to deal with a tendency to panic; all sufferers have to do is stay away from whatever their phobic trigger is, and there are no panic attacks. If that person who became claustrophobic had not done so, there would still have been that 'free-floating' anxiety in the psyche, giving no warning of the moment it would strike and therefore little chance of avoiding it.

184

Sometimes, phobic reactions are directly linked to some traumatic event in the past; sufferers often believe that they know what started it all in the first place, though research has shown that this knowledge is almost always wrong, even when sufferers are absolutely certain that they are right.

This is one of the reasons it can be difficult to deal with the problem – the subconscious will focus you so sharply on what you *believe* to be the cause that you are unlikely to actually discover the *true* cause without the aid of a professional therapist. It is almost inevitable that any belief about the cause of a phobia is erroneous, because the trauma has been 'buried', hidden from current conscious thought; any memory that is conscious cannot cause this type of response pattern, however certain you might be that it is doing so. If every 'bad' conscious memory produced this sort of reaction, all of us would be running around in panic every day! The phobic response is the result of a *subconscious* reaction, not a *conscious* one.

The true phobia is, actually, quite rare. Many people who believe they have a phobia are actually suffering from severe fear instead – and it is easy to tell the difference. Let us assume the 'phobia' is about flying. A sufferer who could get on the aeroplane if he or she was going to receive a reward of ten thousand pounds when they landed has a severe fear, not a phobia. Phobia are linked in the subconscious to the fear of death; true phobics would not get on the plane even for ten thouand pounds, because they would be absolutely certain that they would never live to collect the money.

Dealing with it

If, after reading the paragraphs above, you know you are suffering from a true phobia, you really should seek out a professional therapist to help you deal with it. If you are not able to visit a professional therapist, you can still possibly achieve good results using the Swish technique described in Chapter Seven, linked to self-hypnosis and intensive work on confidence issues generally.

If, on the other hand, you have discovered that you are suffering from severe fear, rather than a phobia, then using that same technique can produce truly astonishing results – and it is *very* fast in these circumstances, sometimes as fast, in fact, as only *fifteen minutes* or so! Occasionally, you might need to do another session after a little while, but there have been very many instances when fears have been banished for good with this method.

If you find yourself reluctant to admit that what you have is a fear, rather than a phobia, then search inside yourself to find out why you would rather have a difficult problem than an easy one. Find out what your hidden agenda or secondary gain is (see Chapter Ten); this is essential if you are to successfully deal with your fear. Frequently, it is a form of an attention-seeking behaviour. Understand what benefit you gain from the 'phobia' and you will quickly realise that it is a pretty poor swap!

Sleep Problems

The vast majority of sleep problems are not as bad as they seem to be; there is ample research to show that most people with insomnia are actually sleeping for far longer than they believe. It is not at all unusual for people to believe that they simply do not sleep, only to find out, when monitored, that they *are* sleeping, sometimes for as long as four or more hours a night in total!

There are two different basic sleep problems – early or continual waking, and difficulty getting to sleep in the first place. There are certain medical conditions that can cause these problems, but generally they are of psychological origin, one of the causes sometimes being worrying about not getting enough sleep! Getting a medical check-up is always a good idea; once you've been reassured that there is nothing physically wrong, you can proceed to do something constructive in the way of self-help.

First of all, read the sections on stress relief in Chapter Eleven, then the section on putting problems to one side in Chapter Seven, and finally, the relaxation phase of self-hypnosis, in Chapter Eight. These passages will be of help and may even do the trick. Otherwise, use self-hypnosis and give yourself the following suggestions. (Record them if you wish, using 'you' instead of 'I'):

When I lay my head on the pillow and I want to go to sleep, that's the signal for quiet, calm, easy feelings to enter my mind and body... so that I can drift easily into a deep and relaxing sleep, waking only when I need to or when I want to.

All my troubles and fears will be resolved at night in my dreams, so I wake up each morning refreshed, relaxed, full of energy and looking forward to whatever new opportunities the day is going to bring.

Repeated use of these two suggestions will almost certainly result in a comfortable sleep pattern in a very short time.

If you prefer more practical methods, then try counting slowly backwards from one hundred down to three; more often than not, you will fall asleep long before you complete that small task. Another method is to imagine yourself going down a very long escalator that passes through several floors of a large building. On each floor you come to, there are fewer and fewer people, everything becomes quieter and quieter, until eventually, there is only you, *completely relaxed*. As you go down one more floor, you find yourself becoming sleepier and sleepier, and you are delighted to find that the next floor is full of the most comfortable, most luxurious beds you have ever seen. You lower yourself onto the nearest bed and just drift into a deep and relaxing sleep. And while you sleep, you have a dream. You dream you are going down a very long escalator...

Bad Habits *(overeating, smoking, etc.)*

Habits respond very easily to hypnotic intervention, even semi-addictive habits like smoking cigarettes. Yes, you did read *semi-addictive*, because *there is no addictive substance whatsoever* in tobacco smoke.

This has been disputed many times, yet no scientist has yet discovered a clinically addictive substance in tobacco smoke. It contains well over four thousand substances, including hydrogen cyanide (used in gas chambers), acetone, propane, embalming fluid and ammonia, but nothing addictive. The oft-repeated statement that 'It has been proven that cigarettes are addictive' leaves out a very important word: that word is 'psychologically'. It *has* been proven that cigarette smoking is *psychologically* addictive. But another name for a psychological addiction is... a habit!

Nicotine, the substance that most people believe to be addictive, is actually a dangerous toxin. It is also a stimulant and can *never* relax you; it has been proven over and again, by the use of stress-monitoring equipment, that smokers become *more* tense after a cigarette than they were before they lit up. You might be protest-ing that you definitely feel more relaxed after a cigarette, but that is simply the belief system at work – have another look at Chapter Five if you have forgotten about the power of the belief system. All your vital signs *prove* you are more tense: your blood pressure is raised, your breathing is faster, your heart rate is faster, and your body temperature drops.

If you doubt that cigarettes are not addictive, consider the follow-ing: if you induce sleep in drug addicts, when they wake up they will have to have however much of their drug they would have had while they were asleep, in order to function. A twenty-a-day smoker, after six to eight hours of sleep, usually has just *one* ciga-rette, even though he or she has missed at least *eight* smokes.

There are many other proofs that cigarettes are, merely habit-forming, not addictive. Perhaps the most obvious is that after hypnotherapy to quit, most individuals simply stop, with no with-drawal symptoms at all. This is often after just one session, though some therapists prefer to do more. Hypnosis to treat individuals for say, heroin addiction, is considerably less effective, and there are almost always pronounced withdrawal effects.

Use self-hypnosis and tell yourself repeatedly: *With each day that passes now, I am leaving the smoking habit further and further behind me... I am no longer a slave to a suffocating and poisonous habit... I am becoming fitter and healthier and more attractive to others with every day that passes.*

Give yourself this message every day for a week, and at the same time see yourself looking healthier and more attractive. If you really want to quit, you will do so easily and completely before a week is through.

You can self-treat other habits in a similar way, giving yourself first a suggestion that you will break the habit easily, secondly reminding yourself of the benefits of doing so. Read the above suggestion again in order to understand this format more clearly.

Overeating is known to be more difficult than most other habits. Some discipline really is needed here, and you will probably need the help of a qualified therapist. In the case of obesity, always seek medical advice first.

Blushing

Like many other personal difficulties, blushing is self-cycling. Because you are afraid that you will blush under certain circumstances, you focus on the idea of blushing – then that is exactly what happens! To the sufferer, the feeling of heat is as bad as, or worse than, the knowledge that they are reddening; it also makes the blush feel much worse than it actually ever is.

Work on confidence issues generally and visualisation in which you see yourself looking cool and calm in situations that used to make you blush. See yourself looking exactly as you *want* to be, not as you are *afraid* you will be. If you are going to think about it at all, you might as well think about what you actually want to happen, because it takes the same amount of effort to think one thing as it does to think another. Self-hypnosis is a first-class tool for helping with this problem. And if you ever feel a blush starting, simply think about being cool, rather than about blushing.

Obsessive Behaviour

This is almost always stress-related and sometimes linked to depression. It is born out of an urge to make sure that everything is safe and secure, that there are no hidden dangers lurking to harm you or people around you, and tends to be episodic, often retreating almost completely for a while. Occasionally, a guilt complex is involved. The best self-help method is daily relaxation or stress-relief exercises as shown in Chapter Eleven until the episode passes. Also, work on confidence issues generally. There is no need to wait until your symptoms have gone away before you begin to pursue success directly; simply become aware that you *can* get them under control.

Depression

This takes two particular forms – endogenous and reactive. Endogenous depression is sometimes referred to as 'clinical' and is somewhat resistant to self-help. Reactive depression is the result of a traumatic, sad or disturbing event; it is the easiest form of depression to treat and the most responsive to psychotherapy.

Working on confidence and well-being generally can be of use, but if the depression is deep-seated and long-lasting, you need professional assistance; seek medical advice first. Results that are little short of amazing can be achieved through psychotherapy and/or hypnotherapy, even where there has been a diagnosis of a clinical condition. If your depression is constant, not altering from one day to the next, no matter what, you are actually suffering from melancholia and you *must* seek medical help.

Depression is often caused by repressed or suppressed anger which has been turned inwards; this situation would need to be identified and resolved before proper relief can be found.

Migraine

The best way to deal with this problem is to tackle it as soon as possible. Recognise your early warning signals, then treat it as you would stress or anxiety. Often fifteen minutes spent in this type of self-help can alleviate much of an attack.

Shyness

Really a form of what is now sometimes called 'social phobia', shyness responds very well to all sorts of self-help interventions.

In fact, just the decision to do something about it is often enough to produce an improvement. The biggest problem with shyness is that, like all self-cycling conditions, it worsens when you focus on it – and when it worsens, you focus on it even more. Some people find they 'grow out of' shyness as they get older.

The best way to treat shyness is to work on confidence issues generally, along with a suitable action VMI. See yourself looking calm, relaxed, confident and popular in all sorts of different situations; there is no need to restrict yourself to situations that you know you will experience. Most shy people are introverted. Most introverted people tend to be thoughtful, self-aware, and, ultimately, intelligent. Most intelligent people have a vivid imagination if they care to use it, and in fact it is imagination that causes most of the problem here – imagining what people *might* be thinking about you. Well, you can use that powerful imagination to banish the problem completely. Read the section on 'The Negative Thinker' in Chapter Ten for more help.

Timidity

This problem usually stems from over-protectiveness by either or both parents. Before you can treat it effectively, you need to accept that you are, in reality, no different from the rest of the human race. Nobody is out to get you, except in your own mind; nobody is trying to hold you back; nobody will punish you if you succeed. You have basically the same thought processes, the same desires, the same urges as the rest of the human race. If people have sneered at you in the past, then that was self-inflicted – they have only done so because you remind them of someone... themselves! Because *everybody* is underconfident in some situations (timidity is just a reaction to underconfidence), when you reveal your fears you remind them of a part of them they would rather not acknowledge. So they convince themselves that you are far weaker than they are, then sneer at you to make themselves feel better.

Some people who believe they are timid are actually suffering from shyness; indeed, the two are very similar. Everything in the section on shyness, above, is equally applicable to timidity.

Work on confidence issues generally, and pretend to be confident; creating a VMI of your Nomad archetype will help you to act the part to perfection. It will not be long before you become what you focus on being.

Memory Problems

Some memory problems can have a clinical origin; if you seem to be worsening, or if you feel the problem is particularly bad, seek medical advice sooner rather than later. Some indicators of a *possible* medical cause, if they happen frequently, are:

♦   Forgetting what you went into a room for.
♦   Forgetting what you went into a shop for.
♦   Forgetting what you are supposed to be doing.
♦   Getting lost when in familiar surroundings.
♦   Forgetting the names of everyday objects.
♦   Forgetting the names of people close to you.
♦   Forgetting how to do familiar tasks or perform familiar actions.

If you find that one or more of the above happens to you often, then there *may* be a medical cause at the root of your memory problem. Most of the time, though, memory problems are really concentration problems, because what does not go in cannot come out! Where concentration problems are severe, it is often a symptom of some form of stress, so using the stress-relief routines in Chapter Eleven should help. Also, you could use self-hypnosis and create a VMI in which you see yourself easily giving full concentration to any situation or subject you choose. This is one of the circumstances where a visit to a professional therapist can produce astonishing results.

Motivation Difficulties

If you do not get motivated, you can be *certain* that you will not become successful. It does not matter how much you *want* success, how much you think you deserve it, or how annoyed you are that you have not yet got it – unless you actually *do* something about it, you will still be feeling the same next year. And the year after, and the year after...

If motivation seems difficult, examine your goals; if they are right, merely looking at them and thinking about how life will be when you have achieved them should be sufficient to get you fired up and eager to get to work. If this does not happen, then either your goals are wrong, or you don't believe that you can achieve them. There is actually a third possibility. It may be that you cannot become motivated for success *because you are already where you want to be, where you 'fit'*. If this is the case, then just sit back and enjoy...

If this is definitely not the case, then you need to work out what is wrong – your goals or your self-belief – and take immediate steps to solve the problem, using the information in this book. Chapters Nine and Ten are relevant and should be of help.

Moodiness

Usually, when most people talk about being moody, they mean being in a 'bad mood' or uncommunicative most of the time. If this is you, then work on confidence, enthusiasm, and optimism issues – but remember your personality group and do not expect to become wildly excited by life or unwaveringly optimistic if you are a Warrior. The Warrior can often seem to be in an irritated or uncomfortable mood, but if this is you *and you are not unhappy within yourself at being like that*, then this is just a predisposition towards seriousness or even sharpness. It is just the way you are and it will in some way contribute to your eventual success. Either of the other groups, though, can make useful changes here, changes that are more in keeping with their basic personality.

Occasionally, when someone refers to moodiness, they mean a tendency toward rapid mood *changes*. If you are a Settler, then this is probably just part of your predisposition, because mood swings are a 'trademark' of this personality type. Working on confidence issues to avoid the 'all or nothing' reaction will minimise it, and this you need to do, because it is one of your negative traits that can serve no useful purpose. The other two groups will find this problem easier to deal with, since it is not part of their major group's behaviour pattern.

Speech Difficulties

Although there may be physical problems associated with speech difficulties, such as birth defects, injury, certain illnesses, or dentition, far more often there are psychological factors are at work. Whatever symptom is evident, be it stuttering or stammering, spoonerisms, halting speech, etc., it always worsens when there is tension because of anxiety or stress. The origins of these problems are usually deep-seated, but they sometimes respond quite well to self-help methods.

Working on confidence issues generally, as well as any self-image problems, can help, as can visualising yourself speaking easily and clearly in a variety of different situations; but by far the most effective self-help method is to *think*. Think what you are going to say before you say it – it only takes a second; think to draw breath before you speak, then think to speak slowly. Make sure you open your mouth properly, rather than mumbling through half-closed lips. Most speech problems will start to diminish if work is done in these areas.

Physical causes are obviously not within the scope of this book, but if there are problems due to dentition, then at least there are simple answers. Some people are aware of spitting when they talk, and this can be quite inhibiting, as well as unpleasant for those on the other end of it. A visit to the dentist is called for: apart from ill-fitting dentures, there are other dental circumstances that can cause this problem.

Jealousy

Although it might be difficult to accept, this is almost invariably due to low self-esteem, so work on confidence issues generally. Jealousy always originates in a subconscious belief that other people have more to offer than you yourself have and are therefore more attractive, likeable, skilled, or whatever. In severe cases, only professional help can bring about lasting change.

Insecurity

Insecurity leads to difficulty in accepting error or in learning from other people, because there is often a continual need to prove oneself worthy in one's own right. It is inhibiting to any form of success; the need to be right all the time prevents the insecure person from taking advice from someone else – that would be an admission of inadequacy, or worse, failure.

Sometimes, there can be a drive to appear 'special' in some way without actually having to do anything concrete to acquire such status (usually Nomad territory); this can involve always having to be 'in the know', inventing tall stories, having a whole host of physical conditions such as allergies or unusual reactions to things, or claiming to have been important or successful in the past.

Chapters One to Eight of this book contain all the information you need to make great and beneficial changes to feelings of insecurity or inferiority.

This part of the book is not intended as an exhaustive exploration of conditions or situations that may have psychological causes. It is simply a guide to self-help for some of the more common of those difficulties. There are many other psychosomatic (created by the power of the mind) and psychogenic (physical illness created by an action of the mind upon the body) conditions, most of which can be speedily, easily, and safely helped by the professional therapist.

Appendix Three
Getting Your Own Way

This appendix shows an advanced way of using the processes you have learned in the main body of the book to be able to handle any personality group with ease.

It is a fact that we all seek to be in control of our life, to get what we want, and in so doing, we often find ourselves in conflict with others. When you have absorbed what is written here, you will be in possession of a wonderful skill that will allow you to find your way through or around such conflicts with ease and elegance. You will not need to get your own way at somebody else's expense – you will get it because they will willingly help you to do so! But this is not about manipulation or in some way being able to fool people; it is about communicating with them on their own terms. It is about creating harmony where there might have been discord.

Each group has a different way of interacting with others, their style of interaction usually being governed by their own personality and attitudes. This means that there is often a good deal of misinterpretation or even a complete misunderstanding. Then objectives, requirements, aims and aspirations get buried beneath a 'clash of personalities'… but it does not have to be this way.

Do you remember this paragraph from chapter seven?

> The Warrior will *use and control* the attributes of the Settler or Nomad.
>
> The Settler will *adapt and modify* the attitudes of the Nomad or Warrior.
>
> The Nomad will *act the part* of the Warrior or Settler.

The phrases in italics can be cthought of as 'psycho switches' that allow you to get the very best out of the resources of each archetype. Later, you will learn how those switches can be programmed to operate *automatically*. First, though, let's analyse how each character deals with others, and the difficulties they might encounter.

Recognition and Understanding

By now you probably have a good feel for each of the personality types; if you have not already done so, it is a good idea to learn, off by heart, the quick recognition guides given in Chapter Two. This will allow you to look at friends, family, work colleagues, acquaintances and even complete strangers and quickly get an idea of what that person is like, what makes them tick. Obviously, other factors come into play, such as intelligence, health and age, environment, social status and so on. Generally, the more intelligent and alert an individual seems, the more noticeably they will reflect the traits that belong to their particular personality type – though it may well be that they exhibit the negative side of their nature.

Each group has its own particular advantage in communication with others, as well as its own particular difficulties. Recognising how and why those difficulties arise leads to understanding; understanding is vital to good communication, and good communication is essential to success, even if that success is simply about getting along with somebody else. The interaction covered in this chapter is relevant to just about every situation *except* life relationships and partners.

It is quite possible, of course, for you to encounter people who behave in a mode that is not truly *them*... just as you may have done before you started to read this book. It is also possible for some people to think in one mode, but behave in another. Both these situations, you are now aware, are because of imprinted behaviour patterns from people's formative years. But we are dealing with behaviour patterns and responses to others here, so, for our purposes, it does not matter one jot whether they are a genuine Warrior, for instance, or have been 'trained' to behave like one.

Many of the suggested behaviour patterns shown here will happen automatically, just as a result of creating your VMI. Placing those changes in your conscious mind by reading about them makes them more powerful and even easier to achieve.

The Settler

The Settler personality is a natural communicator. Settlers like talking, explaining and sharing, and they are attentive when listening, tactful and diplomatic when they need to disagree, and adaptable and open-minded in their dealings with others. Their weaknesses, as far as communication issues are concerned, lie in trying to keep too many people happy at once; their need not to be disliked; their wish not to exploit others or hurt their feelings; and their tendency, sometimes, to lack self-belief.

Dealing with another Settler

Having identified the person you are talking to as another Settler, you can rest assured that they think pretty much in the same way that you do. They will listen to you with an open mind; they will not want to 'put you down' or hurt your feelings in any way; they will want you to be friendly towards them... and they will probably have difficulty in saying 'No'.

More often than not, they will be quite happy to allow you to take charge of the conversation and might actually be more responsive to you if you do so.

When dealing with this personality, you can do no better than to simply be yourself, because their intuitive awareness will straight away see through any act you attempt to put on or any stance you might take, and they will cease to have any trust in you or your ideas. Do not put pressure on them; remember their tendency towards feelings of inadequacy and inferiority, and do not take advantage of their difficulty in saying 'No'. Persuasion and, if necessary, explanation, are far superior tools for you to use in resolving any difficulties that may arise here.

Settlers will generally like you, because you reflect something of their own way of being. With this personality group, your skills and instincts give you a tremendous advantage over the other two groups.

Dealing with the Warrior

This is the tricky one for the Settler, because the Warrior is almost the opposite in many ways. Warriors have little anxiety about being liked or disliked; there is an automatic tendency to attempt to get their own way all the time, and, not infrequently, a lack of tolerance towards attitudes or ideas that are different from their own, even though this may not always be obvious at first. This is not something they choose, or even consciously think about – it is just the way the Warrior is. It is the result of complex subconscious processes which have their roots in their Ancestral Memories, the behaviour patterns of their ancestors. If they are a negative type – this will usually show up as a somewhat curt or impolite manner – then you may have to work quite hard to overcome cynicism or suspicion.

You will benefit from understanding that Warriors like everything to be cut and dried, and feel uncomfortable if things are left 'up in the air'; at the same time they feel uncomfortable with any form of hustling for a decision of any sort. Again, this is their ancestral memories at work, this time insisting that they may be vulnerable if they are not fully in control of their situation. Finding yourself in this company, you should create a VMI of your Warrior archetype; this will straight away allow you to feel more at ease and equal to the situation. Then there are many things you can do to remain so.

Slow down your body language. Remember, this is the least animated of the groups, so slow down to match their movements; this is known as pacing in modern psychology and is the fastest way to establish a healthy rapport with Warriors.

Don't talk too fast. Anything that could remotely be considered 'gabbling' can be irritating to the Warrior and may also be viewed as a sign of empty-headedness or lack of confidence.

Allow pauses. Warriors may well not answer questions immediately, nor will they be likely to respond spontaneously to anything. In all but the most casual of conversations, there is almost always a tendency to evaluate what is being said, so if a Warrior falls silent, wait a few moments before you assume there is not going to be a response. But there may well not be a response – Warriors do not have the same need as you to please people.

Do not try to fool them. The Warrior group is the fastest thinking and most perceptive and will see flaws and anomalies in situations long before anybody else. If they catch you out at any time, they will give you little credibility in the future.

Be practical. A feet-on-the-ground approach is needed here, because anything flippant or extreme is not going to be given a favourable reception. A steady and sensible attitude without exaggeration is always going to produce the best result, whatever the situation.

Stay adaptable. Many people will find this group 'difficult', but you, the Settler, are better equipped than most to get on with Warriors, because of your adaptability and your instinctive grasp of people generally.

Adaptability, persistence and insight are all traits that can impress this group – so use them.

Your Settler personality will really come into its own here, as you incorporate the Warrior's own steadiness of thought and action into your behaviour patterns to increase your communicative abilities.

Dealing with the Nomad

The way Nomads behave has a great deal to do with the way their second group has modified the basic personality. 'Pure' Nomads can be difficult to pin down and can often seem 'slippery' to deal with – they may agree cheerfully with everything you say, without having any intention of acting upon it if it does not suit them; they are quite capable of making promises that would be quite impossible to keep, or that they have no intention of keeping. Your intuitive 'feel' for the behaviour of others will often make you uncomfortably aware of this.

If their second group is Warrior, then their manner may be jokily aggressive or boisterous; if it is Settler, then they will come across as extremely friendly and outgoing. In both cases, it is necessary to remember that they have a far more relaxed attitude to life and work than you have, and they value their freedom to change their mind whenever they like.

When you have created the VMI of your Nomad archetype, it should be easy for you to observe the following rules, which will allow you deal easily and successfully with this personality. You will notice that a fair amount of your Settler self is very appropriate here, and you will find the situation far easier than will the Warrior or, indeed, another Nomad.

Be light-hearted. Nomads cannot stand things getting in any way 'heavy'. They want to enjoy life and usually have a good sense of humour, even when things are going wrong. Use your Settler cheerfulness when dealing with them, and everything should go according to plan.

Be 'them-centred'. This character type tends to be interested in their image and the impression they make upon others. Take an interest in their life and in what they enjoy, and you will get along splendidly.

It is almost impossible to overdo the 'interest in them' attitude.

Get agreement now. If you make plans with this personality type, it is best to make sure things are completely 'signed, sealed and settled' if you want those plans to come to fruition. Otherwise, just when you think everything is ready to go, you may well find that they have changed their mind, forgotten everything that was said, grown bored by the whole idea, or are simply be nowhere to be found! If you need their agreement for something, or if you need them to do something for you, use your Settler persuasiveness in a light-hearted or joky manner to get them to do it today, otherwise the chances are you will be waiting for ages.

Be concise. Nomads can have a short attention span for anything that is not dynamic, so you need to impart the greatest amount of information in the shortest time. You should also find some new and genuinely interesting or exciting angle to work with, because this will grab and hold their attention.

Be enthusiastic and expansive. Use a lively approach in all your dealings with this personality type and bring humour into the situation where you can. Exaggerate, because they will expect it and make allowances for it. If you say that something is 'ten times more likely...' they will think *twice* as likely. If you say 'a hundred times more effective...' they will accept *very much* more effective. If you say 'big' they will think *average*; if you say 'massive' they will think *big*. To make them think *massive*, you would probably need to use a joky word like 'humongous'.

Remember, the comments above are generalisations and guidelines, and should not be taken as absolutely definitive. Trust your Settler *intuition to fine-tune your responses to each group, using your own archetypes – but bearing in mind that any one individual may be only* inclined towards *the behaviour and thought patterns described..*

The Warrior

Warriors are natural 'take-charge' people, the ones who can almost always find a way to be in control of a situation. There is generally a high level of self-belief and an enviable speed of thought which makes it easy to spot opportunities and take advantage of them. This is usually accompanied by a no-nonsense attitude, and a forthrightness and determination in dealing with others, which often leads to Warriors getting their own way. They are unsurpassable when it comes to single-mindedness and tenacity.

Warriors are charming when they need to be and can sometimes seem friendly enough to be mistaken for a Settler personality. This is generally when they have learned that if they are friendly, people will like them, and if people like them, they will get their own way more easily. Often, of course, they *are* genuinely friendly – while things are going their way. It is when they run into opposition that their Warrior determination really shows.

Weaknesses in communication are a tendency to inflexibility and therefore an unwillingness to compromise (though both these traits may be viewed as strengths by some) as well as difficulty in respecting the fact that viewpoints other than their own may be equally valid.

Dealing with another Warrior

The biggest difficulty for you here is that you are confronted with another individual who is just as forthright, just as quick-thinking, just as determined to be in charge of the situation as you are! If you are to get what you want out of your dealings, you will need to remind yourself that confrontation is not the way to do it. Bring your natural manipulative tendencies into play here, using them on yourself *or* the other party, turning the situation around until you can find agreement. This is not backing down or giving in; it is simply using your skills to get at least *something* of what you want, instead of *none* of it.

Your ability to present ideas and concepts in a logical and organised manner will be very agreeable to other warriors and gives you an advantage over the other two groups.

Dealing with the Settler

The easiest mistake to make when dealing with this highly complex personality type is to assume that they are easy to deal with. Easy going they may be, responsive and agreeable, going along with your ideas and concepts and showing interest in all the right places. But upset them or offend them and they will simply shut down and become totally immovable – and you may not even realise this has happened. Under pressure, they will lapse into the 'all or nothing' mode that is so characteristic of the type when they cannot have what they want. Then, they can become uncharacteristically stubborn and refuse to have any further dealings with you at all.

As soon as you recognise the type, create a VMI of your own Settler archetype. Then the following points will help you handle them successfully.

Make friends. Settler types are essentially friendly people and respond well to a comfortable, relaxed, sociable approach. They react badly to the hard sell, the dynamic thrust; under these circumstances, they may go along with your plans, sign orders, contracts, whatever – and then cancel everything without explanation the very next day.

Smile. Settlers want to be liked. Smiling may not always come naturally to your own personality group, but it is certainly easier if you recognise that it will lead to where you want to be. A Settler who believes that you like him will warm to you and be as responsive as only this personality type can be.

Be honest. Where you have a speed and clarity of thought which can be dazzling at times, Settlers have intuition that is almost eerily accurate; they are likely to *know* if you are lying to them, even before you have finished speaking. They may not actually say anything – they are not keen on confrontation – but you will get nowhere at all from that moment onwards.

Be interested. Remember, this is *the* sociable animal – ask them questions about themselves, family, pets, hobbies, etc., and show interest when they reply. Treat them as friends and they will be friends.

Gentle persuasion. As much as this group hates the hard sell, they respond positively to the friendly approach and gentle persuasion. With a bit of care, you will have them eager to please. If they feel that they are doing you a favour in some way, you will be able to rely on their support, as long as you do not abuse it.

Trust them. Settlers are usually honest to a fault. It may sometimes seem to you that they are 'shooting you a line', but you should *never* reveal that thought in any way if you want to keep charge of the situation. Whether they are or whether they are not, showing your disbelief will almost certainly trigger negativity.

Settlers will view you as someone who is positive and determined and knows what he or she is doing – if you get it right. They will see you as overbearing and dictatorial if you don't.

Dealing with the Nomad

This is the most difficult group for you to deal with, for they can seem empty-headed and sometimes even ridiculous, lightweight, and irritating. They are not necessarily so, but they can easily seem so to your practical and down-to-earth personality. They can be almost impossible to pin down and the harder you try, the more determined will they become to avoid doing what you want. At the merest sign of your irritation, however, they will simply change the subject. It is even possible to end up with two conversations at the same time – yours and theirs, with neither of you responding to the other. Like you, they may not be particularly bothered about upsetting people.

They are not particularly people-oriented, but you can successfully deal with them in the same way as you would the Settler – you can create a VMI of either your Settler or Nomad archetypes to help you get it right. The only two differences are:

1. They may not be as honest as Settlers. It is not that they deliberately set out to lie, as a rule; it is more that they tend to get carried away with their own enthusiasm. They will be far less concerned if you challenge them, though – most of them are used to that and they will be likely to laugh off any apparent untruths. Always remember, though, they are consummate actors when it suits them.

2. They will not see you in the same way as Settlers will. Instead, if you get it right, they will view you as a go-getter whom they can respect; if you get it wrong, they may see you as either boring, or a bombastic bully (do not forget their tendency to exaggerate) to be avoided in future.

Do not forget that what is written here is only a guide – it is obviously ridiculous to suppose that every individual will fit into the stereotypical image presented here. Nonetheless, there will always be a distinct leaning towards the listed characteristic responses.

The Nomad

The *Nomad* personality is the lively and enthusiastic communicator who can be either astonishingly impressive or appallingly ineffective – but always enthusiastic and often getting away with far more liberties, by sheer force of personality, than either of the other two groups ever can. When it comes to a dynamic and lively approach, Nomads have no equal and can be relied upon to both entertain and persuade others to their bidding, often with a lot of good humour.

That's on a good day. On a bad day, the Nomads' attributes of boasting, carelessness and lack of attention to detail can begin to show, and they can seem crass and boorish. They are not necessarily so, but that is how they can come across.

Dealing with another Nomad

It is quite likely that you will take a dislike to this competitor for attention, viewing them as childish or a show off! And it is quite possible that they will be viewing you in exactly the same light.

In reality, though, you have a distinct advantage over the other two groups when it comes to dealing with this type. Make sure that what you talk about and the way you talk about it genuinely impresses you and inspires you, and you should be home and dry. The only difficulty you might experience is in tying this mirror image of you down to a firm decision if it is necessary, but as long as you don't expect a higher level of commitment to the proceedings than you yourself would give, you should find your natural enthusiasm and tendency towards humour standing you in good stead.

Dealing with the Settler

You may overwhelm this personality with your natural exuberance, but the adaptable nature indigenous to this group will often have them matching – or attempting to match – your enthusiasm and humour. Get on the right side of them and they will be impressed by your liveliness, inspired by your energy, and happy to go along with your plans as long as there is no direct conflict with their own interests. But watch out for that 'all or nothing' reaction. Settlers are sensitive and uncannily inutuive, and if they feel in any way that you are not taking them seriously, or begin to feel that you are secretly laughing at them for some reason, then they will shut down completely and refuse any further negotiation.

To get the best out of any situation involving contact with the Settler, first, of course, create a VMI of your Settler archetype (and make it as vivid as only a true Nomad knows how!) and follow these guidelines.

Listen when they talk. It is essential for you to be interested in what Settlers have to say; they sometimes tend to suffer from inferiority complexes, and not taking notice of them will not help you. For the same reason, never make fun of something they have said in all seriousness. Also, be sure to let them finish what *they* are saying before *you* speak.

Think hard about their suggestions. Although not as dynamic or inventive as you probably are, Settler's have insights and sudden flashes of inspiration that can be nothing short of amazing. And since they are people-oriented, their ideas may well be highly beneficial to you.

Disagree politely. You may well have a habit of simply brushing aside any idea that does not fit what is already in your mind. You know it is because you have already considered it and dismissed it as not suitable for your needs, but it can come across as if you believe the other person's input to be worthless. At least indicate that you're pondering the idea, then give a valid reason for rejecting it. This will help to keep a Settler very much on your side.

Don't be loud. To Settlers, loud speech, especially if you cut across the end of whatever *they* want to say, feels like an attempt to steamroller them into acceptance of your ideas. They are usually well aware of their tendency to be over-obliging, and this sort of behaviour will put them very much on their guard. They will back-pedal from that moment on.

Do your homework. Whatever idea you are presenting to a Settler, make sure that you are fully conversant with every single aspect of it. If there is the tiniest weakness in your presentation, or in your communication of an idea, the infallible intuition that Settlers almost always posses ensures that they will *feel* that something is amiss. Once they have become suspicious, their basic lack of confidence will cause them to think twice (or even three times) before they make any firm decisions.

Overall, the Settler *personality is likely to view you as a fun person who can be relied upon to brighten up the day and promote a cheerful atmosphere. Or you may be seen as someone who is loud and devoid of substance – the 'empty vessel who makes the most noise'. It's up to you which they see!*

Dealing With The Warrior

The best possible advice for dealing with this type is… do not! The greater the percentage of Warrior the other person has, and the greater percentage of Nomad you have, the more difficult it will be to find any common ground. Unless, that is, you can employ a skill which is an especial quality of your group:

Become an Actor – with a capital A.

Create a VMI of your Warrior archetype and be sure to absorb the feelings associated with the relevant attributes. Then act in a sensible, practical, down-to-earth manner… but do not expect any gratifying response from a Warrior, because he or she simply will not give it. You will be hard put to know whether you are having any effect at all, in fact, and there is little you can do other than communicate what you need to in as rational and organised a way as you can possibly manage.

There are no particular pointers for this group, though all those given in the Settler section on dealing with the Warrior are valid; so, too, are several of those given in this section for dealing with the Settler. It will be obvious which ones when you read them again. The main thing to remember is that Warriors *must* feel in control of the situation at all times and cannot abide anything that smacks of foolishness in any way. That can include excessive enthusiasm, loud humour, expansive and sweeping statements, and exaggeration – all things to which you may sometimes be prone.

Get it right, and Warriors will think of you as a novel and innovative individual and will admire you for it. They will secretly be impressed by your light-heartedness and may even envy it. Get it wrong, though, and Warriors will not think anything of you at all. Nothing complimentary, that is…

Never assume that any individual you are dealing with is going to conform absolutely to the reactions mentioned here. The best thing is simply to recognise that there is a tendency towards that behaviour, then use common sense and whatever intuition you can muster to help you.

Switching Modes

Have yet another look at these statements:

> The Warrior will *use and control* the attributes of the Settler or Nomad.

> The Settler will *adapt and modify* the attitudes of the Nomad or Warrior.

> The Nomad will *act the part* of the Warrior or Settler.

They can be read in two different ways. Taking just the first one, it might mean that the Warrior will use and control the attributes of his or her own Settler or Nomad archetypes; or it might be saying that the Warrior will use and control the attributes and attitudes of the Settlers or Nomads that he or she comes into contact with – in other words, attempt to use and control the other person instead of him or herself. There is a similar double possibility for the Settler and the Nomad, too – he or she will either act the part of their own archetype, or start to mimic or echo the other individual.

This double meaning is actually of great benefit, because it allows the part of each phrase in italics to be used as a 'psycho switch' for you to change modes. It is an easy task; just as soon as you become aware that somebody is trying to get *control* of the situation between you, create a VMI of your Warrior archetype. If they seem to be *modifying* (or *altering*) some of what you say (usually in order to soften it in some way), then your VMI will be that of the Settler. And, of course, if they seem to be *acting a part* in some way, it is the Nomad attributes that you need. To make these switches work automatically, so that the relevant archetype flashes through your mind almost without you realising it, you simply link it up to how you might feel at any time. This can easily be accomplished by using the concentration enhancer or self hypnosis linked to a modified version of the SWISH technique shown at the end of chapter seven. The 'moment of anxiety' would become the recognition of a behaviour – *controlling*, *acting*, or *modifying* – and the 'moment of achievement' would be a VMI of the relevant archetype.

The advantage of using psycho switches like this is that your mode of behaviour can constantly tune itself to the mode of anybody with whom you are in contact – even if they change modes themselves. It will bring about subtle changes that are invisible to anybody other than the most observant people-watcher, who would simply be impressed at your ability to enter another individual's mode of behaviour so easily and accurately. With practice, you will become so skilled that it will seem to others that you just simply have the knack of getting on well with anybody (just like those lucky individuals who already know how to do this without having to learn it in the first place). It will even begin to seem that way to you, too!

Bibliography

Anne Anastasi (1988). *Psychological Testing*, 6th Edition, Macmillan, London.

Richard Bandler (1985). *Using Your Brain for a Change*, Real People Press, Moab, Utah.

Paul Barret *et al.* ed. (1987). *Charles Darwin's Notebooks: 1836-1844: Geology, Transmutation of Species, Metaphysical Enquiries*, Cornell University Press, Ithaca, NY.

Allen E. Bergin & Sol L. Garfield eds. (1994). *Handbook of Psychotherapy and Behaviour Change*, John Wiley, Chichester, West Sussex.

Robert Dilts, Tim Hallbom & Suzi Smith (1990). *Beliefs: Pathways to Health & Wellbeing*, Metamorphous Press, Portland, Oregon.

Dave Elman (1964). *Hypnotherapy*, Westwood Publishing, Glendale, California.

J. C. Flugel (1948). *The Psychoanalytic Study of The Family*, Hogarth, London.

Sigmund Freud (1991). *Introductory Lectures on Psychoanalysis*, Penguin, London.

Stephen Jay Gould (1999). *The Book of Life*, Ebury Press, London.

Donald Johansen & Maitland Edey (1981). *Lucy: The Beginnings of Human Kind*, Paladin, London.

C. G. Jung (1983). *Memories, Dreams, Reflections*, Fontana, London.

Gregorio Kohon ed. (1986). *The British School of Psychoanalysis: The Independent Tradition*, Free Association Books, London.

David G. Myers (1995). *Psychology*, Worth Publishers, NY.

Angela Richards ed. (1991). *Sigmund Freud: The Psychopathology of Everyday Life*, (trans. Alan Tyson), Penguin Books, London.

Abraham P. Sperling (1982). *Psychology Made Simple*, Butterworth-Heinemann, Oxford.

Also by Terence Watts:

Rapid Cognitive Therapy
The Professional Therapist's Guide To Rapid Change Work
Georges Philips & Terence Watts

As the title suggests, this book presents a brief psychotherapeutic approach to working with clients. What it doesn't tell you is that this book reaches way beyond a description of principles and outline of methods and techniques, to provide an easy-to-understand technology for all. Nearly all the techniques here can be used as adjuncts to conventional behaviourist and analytical approaches to therapy including NLP and Gestalt work. As well as describing the art of RCT, the authors have provided the therapist with the means to get started quickly by outlining the structures for the first few sessions as well as giving full scripts for analytical and non-analytical work with the client.

> "Written by two excellent and experienced therapists, [*Rapid Cognitive Therapy* joins] the ranks of modern publications in the domain of psychotherapeutic approaches."
> – *Professor V. M. Mathew, President, British Medical Hypnotherapy Examination Board.*

HARDBACK   **272 PAGES**   **1899836373**